# HISTORICAL CHRISTIANITY AFRICAN CENTERED

James C. Anyike

Other books by James C. Anyike

*African American Holidays*
*Rites of Passage Guidelines*
*Black Love*
*You Gonna Be a Preacher*
*The Faith to Love*
*Bloodied by the Journey*
*One Love*

# HISTORICAL CHRISTIANITY AFRICAN CENTERED

James C. Anyike

Popular Truth Publishing
Indianapolis, IN

Popular Truth Publishing
Indianapolis, IN
www.PopularTruth.com
E-mail: anyike@aim.com



First Edition 1994
Revised Edition 2007
Third Edition 2016
Fourth Edition 2023

ISBN: 978-1-958738-19-1

Cover Design and Layout by James C. Anyike
based on the original design by Troy Brown

Edited by Derrick K. Baker
Printed in the United States of America

## DEDICATED TO

**Mzee Jedi Shemsu Jehewty**
**also known as**
**DR. JACOB HUDSON CARRUTHERS**

As a professor at the Northeastern Illinois University
Center for Innercity Studies,
he was the first to teach me about the
important roles of African Christians in
institutionalizing Christianity.

# CONTENT

# ACKNOWLEDGMENTS

All praises, honor and glory to the Most High God for allowing me to be the vessel through which this book was first written over 22 years ago, and to God's son and servant–Jesus the Christ, who is my older brother, friend, guide and savior.

I thank God for my African and Native American ancestors, through whom the Creator gave me life. I am eternally thankful for my father and mother, Major and Bettie Brame, for passing to me the breath of life and for continuing to save my life each day through their wise sayings and the good Christian up-bringing they provided. I thank Safiyah Fosua for her very profound contribution to this book. I'm thankful for those who have served as teachers and mentors to me, such as Jacob H. Carruthers, Carolyn Knight, Tumani Nyajeka, Mark Ellingson, Randall Bailey, Kwame John R. Porter, Ndugu T'Ofori-Atta, Bishop L. Scott Allen, Bishop Woodie W. White, Al Sampson, Frank N. Moore, Marcus Dixon, Monifa Jumanne, Walter A. McCray, Bill and Ruth Bentley, Ann and Edward Wimberley, Jacqueline Grant, Wilbur Watson, Jonathan Jackson, Carolyn McCrary, Marsha Snulligan Haney, Kwasi Kena, Bishop Julius C. Trimble, Bishop Linda Lee, Calvin Word, James Depp, James Officer, and many others for allowing God to use you to influence my growth and the development of this edition of the book. I am especially thankful to the members of Scott U,M,C. (Indianapolis, IN), The Way (Indianapolis, IN), Christ U.M.C. (Gary, IN), Wesley U.M.C. (Indianapolis, IN), University U.M.C. (Indianapolis, IN), and Fort Street Memorial U.M.C. (Atlanta, GA) for allowing me the privilege to serve as a pastor to you. I'm profoundly thankful for my loving family and good friends who are too numerous to mention. They continue to support, encourage and correct me along the way. Finally, I thank Black Methodists for Church Renewal and the Interdenominational Theological Center (ITC in Atlanta, GA) for the communities of love and support that I have through them. I thank God for guiding me into ministry in the United Methodist Church, and into higher levels of academia, theology and spirituality at Gammon Theological Seminary at the ITC.

# FORWARD

*By Safiyah Fosua*

It has been about forty years, now. More than forty years have passed since the Civil Rights Bill; it has been less than forty years since the assassination of Martin Luther King Jr. Geneticists tell us that a generation ranges between twenty and forty years. So much can happen in a generation. It has been more than a generation since some of our African American children learned what it is like to integrate the neighborhood school. Nearly forty years have elapsed since we began to share control of the education of Black schoolchildren with people who do not share their history. It has been more than a generation since it was legal to send me to the back of the bus.

Exodus tells us that a generation is time enough to forget. Disobedient Israelites were condemned to wander in a wilderness for forty years until the people who held dissenting views died out. But, sometimes, forgetting is not good. What have we forgotten in a generation? Some of our elders, traumatized by the violence of the Sixties, have forgotten to transmit the story of *how we got over* to the next generation. Others, lured by a false sense of equality, or drugged by an opiate dispensed by corporate North America have turned their attention to a neo-bootstraps philosophy that places its energies in obtaining justice for one, instead of justice for all.

We see the fallout in our children—some of whom have become as distant from their cultural heritage as the Second Generation children of North America's Asian and Hispanic communities. This might not be so bad if the world had really changed and racism was a specter of the past. But, to quote 19th Century French journalist, novelist Jean Baptiste Alphonse Karr: *Plus ça change, plus c'est la même chose* "The more things change, the more they stay the same." Karr's epigram reminds us that though many good things have happened, little has changed.

Though forty years seems like a long time, it seemingly is not long enough. Forty years is not long enough for a generation to shed the power of negative images. In 2005, when seventeen-year-old Kiri Davis repeated Kenneth Clark's 1940 doll experiment, she found that preschool and elementary-aged Black children still thought the white doll was good and the Black doll was bad or inferior. Forty years has not been long enough for some of us to absorb the news that the curse of Ham is a misreading of scripture as evidenced by one of my college-aged students in the nineties asking privately "does this really mean that we are not cursed?" Forty years has not been long enough to wipe the N-word out of mouths of both races; nor has it been quite long enough to eradicate racial violence.

The sad truth is that, in far too many places, racism never died, it just went underground for a time to sharpen its skills and has now appeared in the public arena with new vigor and new options. Simultaneous with the retooling of racism has been the wholesale broadcast of mixed messages to an unsuspecting generation. As the façade of unlimited opportunity gives way to the reality that there always was a glass ceiling, our youth and young adults are choosing options other than Christianity to make sense of the world they live in. Gangs and self-destructive behaviors, alternative religious ideologies and irreligion are much more attractive in a climate where people forget who they were and stop talking about who they could be. Keep in mind that a generation has passed since we routinely reminded each other that *we are somebody*!

As we continue to experience the sting of an old enemy wearing new clothes (an enemy to whom some were never formally introduced) it is imperative that Christians of African descent relearn details about our spiritual past. *Historical Christianity African Centered* reveals that we have always been on God's mind. In spite of what the whispers of apartheid theology continue to say about people of African descent, we are not an afterthought, we are in the forefront of Judeo-Christian history. Author James Anyike provides scholarly evidence from careful historical and biblical research that we have been and continue to be prime actors and actresses in the unfolding drama of God's self-revelation to humankind.

*Historical Christianity African Centered* is not an attempt to substitute Black supremacy for white supremacy. James Anyike's work moves us beyond sometimes acerbic tomes of previous generations to embrace the best of Africentric research and scholarship. Reading this revised and expanded edition of *Historical Christianity African Centered* will help us all remember, to borrow a phrase from Dr. Jeremiah Wright, Jr. and the Trinity UCC Church family, to remain "unashamedly Black and unapologetically Christian." As you journey with Rev. Anyike from Noah to Abraham, from Israel to Jesus, from Anthony of the Desert and Pachomius' sister, Mary to the Early Church Fathers and beyond, you will be reminded that Christianity is ours!

**Dr. Safiyah Fosua** writes weekly lectionary-based preaching helps and articles for the United Methodist Church General Board of Discipleship's worship web page (http://www.umcworship.org/). Abingdon Press published her first book, *Mother Wit: 365*

*Meditations for African-American Women* in the fall of 1996 followed by *Jesus and Prayer* in 2002. She is also the associate editor of the *Africana Worship Book*, recently released by Discipleship Resources. Prior to her current appointment as Director of Invitational Preaching Ministries of the General Board of Discipleship, Safiyah and her husband, Dr. Kwasi I. Kena, spent a number of years as missionaries in Ghana, West Africa. Her academic background includes a Doctor of Ministry degree from the United Theological Seminary of Dayton, Ohio, in Afrocentric Pastoring and Preaching.

# INTRODUCTION

Most people throughout the world have been affected in one way or another by Christianity. After nearly 2000 years, the growth of Christianity is similar to a mighty tree with millions of leaves, thousands of branches, and hundreds of stems all connecting to one common stem called the "trunk." Today, Christianity is represented by millions of people, belonging to thousands of congregations that are connected to hundreds of denominations, originating with one common historical figure, Jesus the Christ.

The racism prevalent today in many parts of the world did not exist during biblical times (i.e., 3000 B.C.E. to 100 C.E.). Neither was racism a major factor as the Christian Church developed from the 1st to the 6th Centuries. The Bible gives no clear indication that race mattered among biblical people as a religious, economic, social or political factor. However, racism was imposed on Christianity, and resulted in the belief that biblical people were white.

The physical appearance of Jesus is popularly perceived as Caucasian. This perception also applies to most biblical figures. For many Christians, the acceptance of biblical figures as white is hardly questioned. However, challenges to these false portrayals have escalated as more fair-minded researchers study the historical, anthropological, archaeological, genetic and biblical facts.

It is inconsistent for Christians to present the gospel, or "good news," as a gospel of truth, and yet, not challenge lies told about the central figure that the religion represents. If biblical persons in their true ethnic appearance become unacceptable to Christians because they were Black people, then the believer's racism is more powerful than their faith. One of the earliest known portraits of Jesus is found in the Catacomb of Domitilla in Rome. This 2nd Century portrayal is that of a very dark-skinned man with black hair. In Chapter 6, this matter of Jesus' skin color is dealt with in more detail.

The same false perceptions exist about the founding of Christianity. The biblical record places a great deal of emphasis on the writings and ministries involving Rome and Asia Minor. These canonical scriptures say nothing about the thriving growth of Christianity in Alexandria, Egypt, which may have started as early as 39 C.E.

We have been given the impression that the religion started with a small group of persecuted Jews but was nurtured and spread when the Roman government accepted it after Constantine. An accurate history of early Christianity cannot be presented without inclusion of the African contributions to the religion.

Any historian, who is committed to accuracy, will not hesitate to acknowledge that the Egyptians (or Kemites) of biblical times were Black people; that many of the most highly respected Church fathers were African men; that Christian monasticism was started by an African man; that the first Christian educational institution was started by an African; that African church leaders were at the forefront of every major ecumenical council during the first five centuries of the religion; and that Africans served a most crucial role as translators and preservers of the scriptures.

Through this text, the historical record of early Christianity is made clear and inclusive, reflecting the various ethnic cultures that contributed to it. The information provided herein is not slanted to create false impressions and myths about the roles of Black people in early Christianity. *Historical Christianity African Centered* is presented as a missing link in popular Christian history.

This text has four major parts. In Part 1 the racial compositions of the Israelites and other Hebrew Bible (i.e., Old Testament) people are explored.

**Chapter 1 - The Sons of Noah** examines the close relationships between those considered the descendants of Ham and Shem. Through our examination of the families of Noah's three sons we will identify the close cultural and racial similarities between people classified as "Semitic" and those classified as "Hamitic."

**Chapter 2 - The Children of Father Abraham** examines the interaction that Abraham and his descendants had with different people from Mesopotamia to Egypt. It is interesting to note that Abraham came from an ancient city of the Mesopotamia called Ur, which was in a region that is known to have been populated with Black people at that time. This chapter also presents an examination of the intermixing that took place between Abraham's family and Black Semitic and Hamitic people.

**Chapter 3 - The Israelites Becoming a Kemitic People** explores the making of Israel into an Egyptian people in culture, language and race. According to the biblical text, a small group of about 70 members of Joseph's family joined him in Egypt, and in less than 400 years the children of Israel multiplied to over 600,000 men of military age. Adding children, women and elders to the young men would probably increase the total to over 2 million people during the exodus period. This growth must have involved intermixing with the Egyptians. With more than 99.9% of the Israelites first four generations being born in Egypt, they were an Egyptian people when they left Egypt.

**Chapter 4 - The Israelites Scattered Among the Nations** provides an overview of Israel's interaction with different nations from the exodus period to the time of Persian domination. Despite the laws against intermixing with people that worshiped other gods, many of the children of Israel continued to intermix. Weakened through wars and internal conflicts, the tribes of Judah and Benjamin split from the other ten tribes in 922 B.C.E., producing a separate "Judah" kingdom from Israel. In 721 B.C.E. Israel was conquered by the Assyrians. Samaria, the capital of Israel, became a place of idolatry and mixed heritage, Further subjection to foreign rule, under the Babylonians and Persians, left the children of Israel a shadow of their past greatness when Alexander conquered Palestine in 332 B.C.E.

**Chapter 5 - Greek and Roman Rule Over Israel** presents a historical picture of Palestine from 332 B.C.E. to 1 C.E. This examination of Greek and Roman rule in the Mediterranean region explains the political and social relationships they had with Israel. Herein the Maccabean and Herodian dynasties are introduced, setting the stage for the political climate that existed during the beginning of Christianity.

In Part 2 the history of the New Testament is introduced, with a special emphasis on the race of Jesus, his disciples, apostles and early believers.

**Chapter 6 - The Biblical and Historical Jesus** presents a wide range of sources to show how Jesus was portrayed and perceived in early history. Early portrayals of Jesus are found in Roman catacombs, on a Roman coin, and hundreds of statues and paintings of Jesus and Mary. These depictions generally present Jesus as a young man with a very dark complexion.

**Chapter 7 - Jesus' Disciples and Apostles** is a general introduction to the hundreds of people called disciples of Jesus, and brief biographies of the 12 disciples and apostles that were closest to him. This chapter also presents a historical review of the spreading of Christianity throughout the 1$^{st}$ Century. During the 1st Century there were many conflicts among early Christians and controversies about Gentiles joining the religion and whether they were subject to Jewish laws. The New Testament pays little attention to the efforts of the original apostles of Jesus in spreading the gospel. Most of the emphasis is on the works and writings of Paul. It is interesting to note that Paul had the physical appearance of a particular "Egyptian" according to Acts 21:38. This chapter highlights the efforts to spread the gospel to the people of the Mediterranean region and the persecuting of Christians by the Roman government.

**Chapter 8 - Christianity Institutionalized in Africa** gives special emphasis to what became the strongest community of early Christianity. Because the apostles were Jews, they placed most of their emphasis on converting Jews. There were many Jewish communities outside of Judea. The community of Jews in Alexandria, Egypt was the largest of the Jewish Diaspora. Because Alexandria was only 380 miles from Jerusalem, travel between the two cities was common. It is not likely that the apostles would fail to spread the gospel to Alexandria. According to Coptic tradition, St. Mark (i.e., John Mark) journeyed to Egypt to establish a community of Christians.

In Part 3 the important contributions of Africans to early Christianity are presented. Their contributions to the religion are invaluable. The lack of attention given to this subject by church historians is at least negligent, and at most racist.

**Chapter 9 - Christian and Kemetic Beliefs Compared** compares the ancient Egyptian myth of Osiris (i.e., Ausar) to the biblical Jesus Christ. The myth of Osiris may be over 10,000 years old and many of the attributes ascribed to Jesus Christ were first represented in the myth of Osiris. Attention is also given to biblical references to Jesus as the "chief cornerstone" and "the Amen." Both terms have Egyptian explanations.

**Chapter 10 - Fathers of the Christian Church** gives credit to these African men that are held in high esteem in Christian history but are seldom referred to as "Black" or "African" people. Highly respected are Tertullian as the creator of Christian Latin literature; Cyprian as the source of the episcopalian and papalist views of church order; Origin as an interpreter of orthodoxy, educator, and profound writer; and Augustine as a defender of Christianity, theologian, and Bishop of Hippo.

**Chapter 11 - Christian Education** informs the reader about the first theological institution of Christianity, which is called the "Didascalia" or "Catechetical School of Alexandria." It provided the highest training in Christian thought during the 2nd and 3rd Centuries. Prominent African heads of the school included Clement and Origin. It was at the Didascalia that many profound theological ideas were developed and documented.

**Chapter 12 - Christian Monasticism** is a report of the great leaders of Christian monasticism which began in Egypt in the 3rd Century, started by Antony and Pachomius, both African men. Antony is called "the father of Christian monasticism." Pachomius instituted the cenobitic form of monastic living. Monasticism spread from Africa to the European world. It was also in Egypt that the first convent was founded by Mary, Pachomius' sister.

**Chapter 13 - Preservers of the Scriptures** discusses how the first translations of the Old and New Testaments were made in Egypt. Thanks to African monasteries, many biblical writings were hidden from Roman officials that sought to destroy them. They also preserved writings that were declared heretical. Throughout the 20th Century, many ancient manuscripts were found in Egypt. The most significant find was in 1945 near Nag Hammadi in Upper Egypt.

**Chapter 14 - African Martyrs for Christ** examines the zeal of African Christians that considered it a great honor to die for their faith in Jesus Christ. Most inspiring are the reports of bravery and miracles among the martyrs. The persecution of Christians lasted almost four hundred years throughout the Roman Empire. There were many Christians who were elevated to the status of "saint" by the Church.

Throughout Part 4, a brief history of Christianity after the Council of Chalcedon is presented. The focus of the religion shifted from Africa to Rome, largely due to military and political force.

**Chapter 15 - The 1st Great Schism of Coptic and Catholic** provides brief histories of these two churches after they split. Special emphasis is given to the Coptic Church history.

**Chapter 16 - How Christianity was Colored White** shows how history was distorted to produce the false perception that the people of the Bible were white. In 1505 Pope Julius II commissioned Michelangelo to paint a portrait of Jesus. White images of the biblical figures created by Michelangelo have become popularly accepted as historically accurate. Motion pictures about biblical events have instilled deep mental images in our minds that Moses looked like Charlton Heston (an American actor) and spoke an old English dialect. Herein, we challenge the use of these false images.

**Chapter 17 - Christianity Reclaiming its Africentrism** is a challenge to Christians to accept the truth about African contributions to Christianity. For more than 500 years Black Christians have accepted false portrayals of biblical figures as white. Can Christians of all races now accept true Black portrayals of biblical figures and are they prepared to expect the return of Jesus as a Black man?

It's interesting to note that there are many Africentric (or Afrocentric) thinkers who have been convinced that Jesus never existed, or that Christian theology was shaped by Emperor Constantine at the Council of Nicea. Both suppositions are wrong, and this book shows why.

It is likely that this information will be considered racist by a few people. Since it was first published in 1995, until this $4^{th}$ Edition, it has gained wide acceptance in seminaries, churches, and homes across color lines. This text is not a replacement of white racism with Black racism. Before it is judged negatively, one important question must be answered. The question is, "Is this a truthful and accurate portrayal of history based on reliable historical, biblical and archaeological sources?" If the answer is "No," then it must be objectively challenged in order to produce a more historically accurate report. If the answer is "yes," it must be accepted and respected as a valid contribution to the historical record of the Church. It is a confirmation of the old sayings "Truth crushed to earth will rise again," and "The truth will make you free."

*Chapter 1*

# THE SONS OF NOAH

The book of Genesis reports that Noah was commanded by God to build an ark that would be used to save the earth's animals and Noah's family from a flood. The people who entered the ark were Noah, his wife (whose name is not given), his three sons Japheth, Shem and Ham, and his son's wives (whose names are not given).

Accordingly, these were the people who survived the flood and fruitfully multiplied to replenish the earth. The race of Noah's family is not stated in the Bible. Yet, a biblical and historical study of those people who are identified as descendants of Noah's sons will lead to a clearer conclusion about their race.

The focus of this chapter is on Shem and his descendants, leading up to Abraham in about 1800 B.C.E. It is from Shem that the children of Israel come to be.[1]

According to the 11th chapter of Genesis, the survivors of the flood traveled east and settled in Shinar. The Bible reports that the ark rested on Mount Ararat. For hundreds of years there have been many reported sightings of the ark on Mount Ararat.[2] Before they traveled east, we learn from the 9th chapter of Genesis about Noah planting a vineyard, getting drunk from wine and falling asleep naked. Ham, Noah's young son (הַקָּטָן in Hebrew) does not refer to being the youngest son, but used to describe size or

---

[1]There are four terms that must be defined to give us a better understanding of who the children of Israel are. The terms are *Semite*, *Hebrew*, *Israelite* and *Jew*. A Semite is any person who descended from Shem. A Hebrew is any descendant from Heber (also Eber), a great-grandson of Shem. The name Israel refers to Jacob, Abraham's grandson. Israelites are the descendants of Jacob. A Jew is any person or descendant of the tribes of Judah and Benjamin, which split from the other 10 tribes.

[2]Tim LaHaye and John Morris, *The Ark on Ararat.* New York: Thomas Nelson Inc., Publishers, 1976. *National Geographics*, "Noah's Ark Found in Turkey? By Nat Than. April 30, 2010, http://news.nationalgeographic.com/news/2010/04/100428-noah-ark-found-in-turkey-science-religion-culture/

significance, not age), found his father in this condition and reported it to his brothers. Subsequently, Noah was angry with Ham and cursed Canaan, Ham's son. The reason for his anger is not clear, nor is it clear why Canaan was targeted rather than Ham and/or all of his sons.

Some historians and theologians have used this story to justify the African slave trade. Those who supported slavery argued that the proper station in life for Blacks was to be "hewers of wood, drawers of water" and servants to the white race.[3] It is interesting to note that this racist explanation of the curse concedes that the Canaanites are Black people. The Israelites often intermixed with the Canaanites, as will be proven in the following chapters.

Even more puzzling is the story of the Tower of Babel in the 11th chapter of Genesis. From this story we learn that sometime after they settled in Shinar, God "came down to see the city and tower" the people built. God became displeased with their abilities of communication and imagination. For this reason, God "confounded" their language so they could not understand each other and "scattered" them across the earth.

These stories may be metaphoric representations of how people were spread throughout the world. The author has no intentions to prove or disprove the veracity of these stories. The reader may choose to view them as historical, biblical or mythical accounts of how the earth was replenished and how people were scattered throughout the world. They are used herein to provide biblical references to the more historically verifiable accounts of the existence of the Jews, which led to the establishing of Christianity.

After the "scattering," the descendants of Japheth are seldom referred to in the Bible. According to Genesis 10:3-5 the descendants of Japheth are Gomer, Magog, Madai, Javan, Tubal, Meshech, and Tiras. It also states that the descendants of Gomer are Ashkenaz, Diphath, and Togarmah, and the descendants of Javan are Elishah, Tarshish, Kittim, and Rodanim. The descendants of Japheth are referred to as "coastland peoples," "Isles of the Gentiles," or "coastlands of the nations." It is interesting to note that all of the descendants of Japheth are only mentioned in the genealogies or in apocalyptic prophesies of the Bible, with the exception of Tarshish. In the genealogies (Genesis 10 and 1Chronicles 1) Tarshish is identified as

---

[3]Eric L. Mckitrick, editor, *Slavery Defended: The Views of The Old South*. Englewood Cliffs, NJ: Prentice-Hall, Inc., 1963, pp.86-98.

Japheth's grandson. This is the only place where this name is used to identify an individual. The other uses of the name refer to a place. It was to Tarshish that Jonah went to avoid God's call. The location of Tarshish is not known. Therefore, we cannot know what the people of Tarshish were like. The children of Ham and Shem had practically no interaction with their Japhethite relatives.

Shem is the ancestor of the Semitic people. He had five sons and three of these are the ancestors of tribes with identified geographical locations. Elam produced the Elamites, Asshur produced the Assyrians and Aram produced the Arameans (also called Syrians). Shem's son Arphaxad was the grandfather of Heber. It is from Heber that the Hebrew tribe is produced. No geographical location is identified for this tribe.

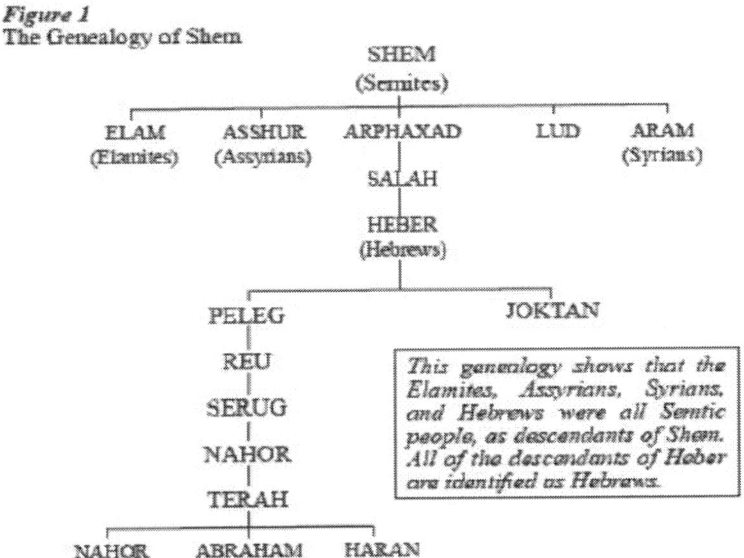


For many years historians used three classifications to group the people of the earth according to similarities in language, religion and appearance. The classifications were Hamitic, Semitic and Japhetic.[4] In general, the Hamitic people were regarded as Black Africans (or Negroid); the Semitic people as Asian (or Mongoloid); and the Japhetic people as white Europeans

---

[4]Walter Arthur McCray, *The Black Presence in the Bible.* Chicago: Black Light Fellowship, 1990, p. 41 and H.G. Wells, *The Outline of History,* New York: The MacMillan Company, New York, 1921, p. 110.

(or Caucasoid). Subsequently, the association of Hamitic people with Blackness was changed to include white people. This was probably done by historians who could not accept the fact that the first and greatest civilizations (i.e. Egyptian and Mesopotamian) were Black civilizations. Historians differentiated the Hamites from the so-called "Negroes" in western and southern Africa. Accordingly, the Egyptians, Ethiopians and Mesopotamians were described as "dark-skinned whites," "dark red," "copper colored," "brown," "whites with black skin," "Mediterranean," "Eurafrican" or "Caucasoid Blacks."[5] However, it has been proven that the people of these great civilizations were basically the same as the rest of the people of the African continent, having dark (or black) skin, thick lips, broad noses and kinky black hair.[6]

The ancient Semites are closely associated with the Hamites in language, religious beliefs and most often in appearance. The Hebrew language is related to that of the Canaanites. Many philologists agree that there are connections between the Semitic and Hamitic languages, but neither closely connect to Aryan tongues. Historian H.G. Wells said, "The Semitic languages may have arisen as some specialized proto-Hamitic group."[7] Sumerian is the oldest written language known. This Hamitic tongue, used by the Mesopotamian civilization of Sumer over 6,000 years ago, is used by philologist as the foundation for the study of the development of languages.[8]

Like Hamitic people, the Semites also engaged in worship of the sun and fertility (or phallus) symbols. The ancient Hebrews also engaged in dice throwing, sacrificing to idols and worship of the sun god Bel. Terah, Abraham's father, and his contemporaries were known to have "served other

---

[5]Cheikh Anta Diop, *The African Origin of Civilization,* Westport: Lawrence Hill & Company, 1974, Chapter 3.

[6]Bishop Alfred G. Dunston, Jr., *The Black Man in the Old Testament and its World,* Trenton: Africa World Press, Inc., 1992, pp. 27-33.

[7]Wells, *The Outline of History,* p. 121.

[8]*Insight Magazine,* "Tracking Mother of 5000 Tongues," by Harvey Hagman, February 5, 1990, pp. 54-55.

gods."[9] The worship of idols seemed to come easy to the children of Israel after they left Egypt. The Bible reports that God was prepared to destroy them when they made a golden calf and began worshiping it. Aaron's excuse to his brother Moses for the idolatry was "you know the people, that they are bent on evil."[10] Dr. Charles Finch, III, asserts that the exodus of the Israelites from Egypt resulted from their worship of the god Set after worshipers of Amen gained power in Egypt.[11]

Geographically, the descendants of Shem are always found in lands with, or close to, Hamitic people, as was the case with the descendants of Elam living with the Sumerians. Approximately 180 miles north of the Persian Gulf was the ancient city of Susa, which was the capital of Elam. It was one of the earliest historic civilizations of high culture and sat on the eastern border of Sumer. It dates back to about 3000 B.C.E. and is often compared to the Nile Valley civilization of Egypt. The Elamites developed copper weapons, cultivated grain, domesticated animals and had hieroglyphic writings and business documents.[12]

Historical, archaeological and anthropological evidence verifies that these descendants of Elam, one of Shem's sons, were Black. According to Egyptologist Gaston Maspero, the Elamites were "a short and robust people of well-knit figure with brown skin, Black hair...who belong to the Negritic race." English Orientalist George Rawlinson said the Elamites had a "Negro type of countenance," that their heads were "covered with short crisp curls," and that they had "thick lips."[13] Further proof of the Black heritage of Elam is provided through the efforts of archaeologist Marcel Auguste Dieulafoy, who found depictions of Black rulers on panels of enameled bricks from ancient Susa, the capital of Elam (Genesis 10:11).

---

[9]*Holy Bible,* New Revised Standard Version, Grand Rapids: Zondervan Bible Publishers, 1990, Joshua 24:2.

[10]Ibid., Exodus 32:22.

[11]Ivan Van Sertima and Runoko Rashidi, Editors, *African Presence in Early Asia,* New Brunswick: Transaction Books, New, 1988, pp. 190-192.

[12]Will Durant, *Our Oriental Heritage,* New York: Simon and Schuster, 1954, p. 117.

[13]Van Sertima, *African Presence in Early Asia,* p. 20.

About 380 miles northwest of Susa was the land of Assyria. Its major cities included Asshur. Nimrod and its founders were migrants from Babylon. Genesis identifies Ham's son, Nimrod, as its founder.[14] The Assyrians are well known for being the first to equip its large army with iron weapons, and ultimately became an empire dominating Babylon, Palestine, Egypt, and most of the Near East.

The early history of Assyria dates back to about 2300 B.C.E. According to Egyptologist Jean Francois Champollion, examination of bas-reliefs on the tomb of Sesostris I depict images of Asians represented differently from those of the Egyptian and European images. The Assyrian image is described as having "tanned complexion, aquiline nose, Black eyes and thick beard...clad in rare splendor."[15] A 7th Century Assyrian relief from the palace of Ashurbanipal shows Assyrian musicians with broad noses, thick lips, heavy beards and dreadlocks (or a head piece that looks like dreadlocks).[16]

An Assyrian musician depicted in a 7th Century relief from the palace of Ashurbanipal

Syria was located about 355 miles west and slightly south of Nineveh, about 50 miles east of The Great Sea (later called the Mediterranean Sea). Depictions of Syrians found in Egyptian bas-reliefs, and wall paintings, show them with dark skin and features like most African people. A 13th Century B.C.E. painting, which is part of a decoration at the base of the throne of Amenhotep III, shows two Syrians with black hair, thick lips, broad noses and dark skin.[17]

Other images of Black Syrians are found on the ceremonial walking stick

---

[14]*Holy Bible,* Genesis 10:11.

[15]Diop, *The African Origin of Civilization,* p. 47.

[16]Joan Comay and Ronald Brownrigg, *Who's Who in the Bible,* New York: Bonanza Books, 1980, p. 59.

[17]James B. Pritchard, *The Ancient Near East in Pictures.* Princeton: +Princeton University Press, 1954, p. 2.

of Tut-ankh-Amon, the tomb of Horemheb at Memphis, the tomb of Amenemheb at Thebes and a painting of a Syrian warrior from Tell el-Amarna.

Since Semitic and Hamitic people were neighbors, naturally there was interaction between them. At times they engaged in trade, intermixing and war. Based on the archaeological and historical information presented about the Elamites, Assyrians and Syrians, we can conclude that the Black presence among these people was quite prominent. The lack of proof supporting a white presence among these people further justifies this position. If it is true that the descendants of Shem's three sons were Black, then their patriarchs were Black. This gives us good reason to conclude that Shem and his other two sons were Black.

*Chapter 2*

# THE CHILDREN OF FATHER ABRAHAM

Though they were Semitic people, Abraham and his descendants had very close relationships with Hamitic people. In fact, they had more contact with Hamitic people than Semitic people. The integration of Abraham and his descendants with Hamitic people was by choice, in some cases, and commanded by God in others. When Abraham's family is first introduced in the book of Genesis, they were living among Hamites in Ur of the Chaldees.

Acceptance of the belief that the biblical Hamites were Black people is most important in concluding that the early Hebrews were greatly influenced by a distinctly Black people. In general, Hamites are classified as Black, despite the efforts of some historians to classify them as white.[18] The weight of historical and archaeological proof remains on the side of those who support belief in Hamitic Blackness, as will be shown in this chapter.

At this point, it is necessary to identify the Hamites of the Bible and present references that validate their Blackness. Ham, one of the sons of Noah, had four sons. Their names were Cush, Egypt, Put (or Phut) and Canaan. The genealogies of Ham's sons show what nations were produced from them (See figure 1 on page 16).

According to Old Testament scholar Charles B. Copher, "The evidences indicate that, in the main, wherever in the Bible Hamites are referred to they were people who, today in the Western world would be classified as Black, and Negroid."[19] There is much evidence to support the Black heritage of those Hamites of the African continent and Mesopotamian region.

---

[18]Charles B. Copher, *Black Biblical Studies.* Chicago: Black Light Fellowship, 1990, p. 123.

[19]Ibid., p. 36.

*Figure 1*
**The Genealogies of Ham's Sons**

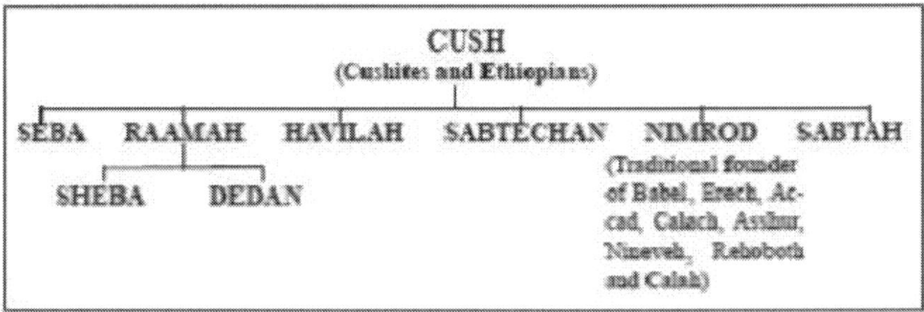


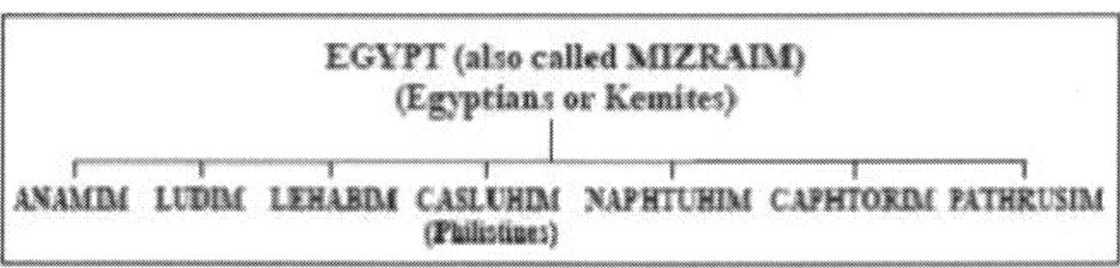


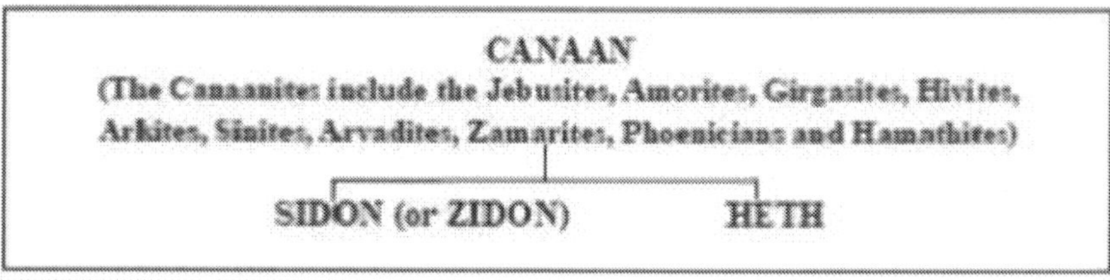


**PHUT**
**(The traditional ancestor of the Libyans or Cyrenes. No descendants are listed in the Bible)**

**According to the Bible, the sons of Ham are Cush, Egypt, Canaan and Phut. These sons and all of their descendants are Hamites.**

The United Nations Educational, Scientific and Cultural Organization (UNESCO) reached a consensus at its Cairo Symposium in 1974, which stated, "There is no evidence that the ancient Egyptians were white, and that Egypt was not influenced by Mesopotamia, but by peoples from the Great Lakes region in inner-equatorial Africa." George Rawlinson `confirms that "the fundamental character of the Egyptian in respect of physical type, language and tone of thought, is Nigritic."[20]

The Blackness of the Cushites is generally accepted with little disagreement. Tribes identified as descendants of Cush are mostly located in Africa and Arabia.[21] African Cushites occupied the regions that are now known as Sudan, Ethiopia and Somalia. The names of these regions "speak for themselves" in verifying their Black heritage. The name *Sudan* means "land of the Blacks" and *Ethiopia* literally means "land of burnt faces."

Nimrod, one of the sons of Cush, is addressed in the Bible as "a mighty one in the earth" and "a mighty hunter before the Lord." He is also identified as the founder of many of the nations in the Mesopotamian region (Genesis 10:8-12). According to Dr. Walter A. McCray, "There are also definite linguistic relationships between Cush, Kish, Cassites (Kassites), and Cosseans. Furthermore, the 'Cush' of this passage is related also to Assyria via Babylonia, Cushite civilization advanced up the Tigris-Euphrates."[22]

A Canaanite traveler as depicted in an Egyptian relief from Horemheb

The Canaanites and the Phoenicians are one and the same. These Hamitic people are said to have "dwelt" in Canaan "of old," according to 1st Chronicles 4:40. They were a peaceful people who inhabited the "land that flows with milk and honey," which was promised to the children of Israel. Since ancient times they were believed to be the inventors of navigation. Cheikh Anta Diop described the Phoenicians as

---

[20]Ibid., p. 29.

[21]Walter Arthur McCray. *The Black Presence in the Bible, Vol.2.* Chicago: Black Light Fellowship, 1990, p. 95.

[22]Ibid., p. 96.

"a Negroid people, more or less cousins of the Egyptians."[23]

The process of identifying the Putites as Black people is less obvious than other Hamitic people. Though no genealogy is given in the Bible for Put, the Libyans are traditionally recognized as his descendants. Flavius Josephus identifies Put as the founder of Libya. Historically, the difficulty in the identification process results from the invasion of the Western region of the Nile Delta by tall, blond, blue-eyed Indo-Europeans around 1500 B.C.E.[24] According to Dr. Jacob Carruthers of the Association for the Study of Classical African Civilization (ASCAC), northern Libya was occupied by white people who the ancient Egyptians called *Tchemehu*. The Egyptians distinguished them from the Black people (who looked like them) of southern Libya called *Tchehenu*.[25] A 12th Century B.C.E. Egyptian glazed tile shows a distinctly Black Libyan. The presence of white Libyans in the region led some historians to believe northern Africa was generally inhabited by a white indigenous population. However, they were Indo-European invaders (or migrants), and not a Putite people like the Black Libyans.

Statuette of a Canaanite goddess

Depiction of a Libyan from a 12th Century B.C.E. Egyptian glazed tile

The question that should be asked at this point is "what contact did Abram (Abraham) and his descendants have with these Black people?" Abram and his family started their journey from Ur of the Chaldeans, a region of Black people that may have been politically dominated by the Cassites (possibly a Cushite people), around 2100 B.C.E.

---

[23]Cheikh Anta Diop, *The African Origin of Civilization Myth or Reality.* Westport: Lawrence Hill & Company, 1974, p. 166.

[24]Cheikh Anta Diop, *The Cultural Unity of Black Africa.* Chicago: Third World Press, 1978, pp. 62-63.

[25]Dr. Carruthers presented this information in a class lecture on African history, which he delivered in 1987 at the Northeastern Illinois University Center for Inner City Studies in Chicago, Illinois.

According to the 11th chapter of Genesis, Terah took his son Abram, his grandson Lot, and Abram's wife Sarai (also Terah's daughter) to go into the land of Canaan. They traveled along the Fertile Crescent, northeast to Haran. Before going south to Canaan, they settled in Haran where they had a home, amassed "substance" (or material wealth), and bought (or hired) servants. Haran was a commercial center in the northern region of Assyria and probably was a place where different nationalities lived. While living there, Terah died.

In chapter 12 of Genesis, Abram is told by "the Lord" to leave his "father's house to [go to] the land that I will show you" where "I will make of you a great nation, and I will bless you. ....I will bless those who bless you, and the one who curses you I will curse." This "promised land" was Canaan, a land inhabited by Hamitic people. They set up a tent in the mountains between Bethel and Hai (or Ai), but soon traveled to Egypt because there was a famine in Canaan.

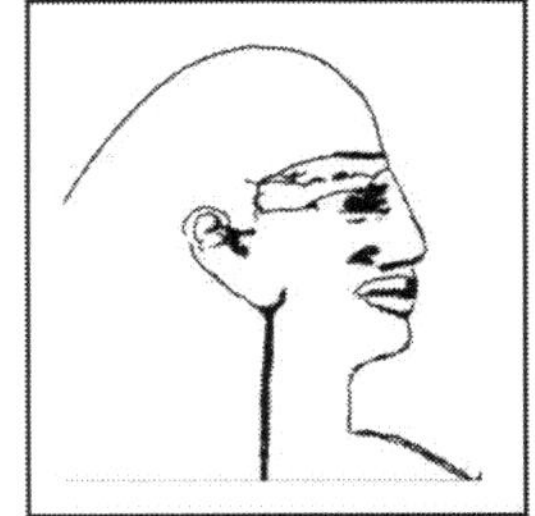
An Egyptian as depicted in a Middle Kingdom relief.

While in Egypt, Abram introduced Sarai as his sister (she was his half-sister, born of a different mother). Though she was about 65 years old, she was described as appealing to the Egyptians and Abram allowed her to be taken into Pharaoh's house. In return, he was given much livestock and many servants. It is strongly implied that Pharaoh and Sarai had sexual relations. This is the first sexual encounter between a Hebrew and Hamite that was reported in the Bible. If there was no sexual activity, there would have been no reason for God to strike Pharaoh's house with a plague.

After leaving Egypt they traveled south (probably to Cush). They then traveled back to Bethel after becoming very rich in silver, gold and cattle. A dispute arose among the Hamitic herdsmen of Lot and Abram. These men were Perizzites and Canaanites. Abram suggested that they separate into different regions so they could live without conflict. Abram remained in Canaan and Lot moved to Sodom.

The location of Sodom and the other cities that shared the region (Gomorrah, Admah, Zeboiim and Zoar) is not known for certain. The five countries were a part of a federation called "the Vale of Siddim" and was probably located along the southeast shore of the Salt Sea (later called the Dead Sea). The region was subject to Elamite rule and rebelled against the king of Elam named Chedorlaomer. Sodom was probably a Semitic country because it was subject to Black Semitic authority in Elam.

The rebellious actions of the Vale of Siddim led to an attack on them by Chedorlaomer and three other kingdoms, which were victorious in ransacking Sodom. Lot was taken captive, which caused Abram to get involved to rescue his nephew. He took 300 men (servants) from his house to defeat Chedorlaomer's forces and rescue Lot. Most of the men with Abram were Hamites. Aside from a few servants who may have joined him in Haran, the rest were Egyptians, Cushites and Canaanites. It is important to note that Abram and Sarai have lived only in Hamite lands after leaving Haran. Therefore, most of their servants naturally would be Hamitic. Abram also received help from three Amorite brothers named Memre, Eshcol and Aner. This is the first biblical report of Hamites and Hebrews joining as allies in war.

After the conflict was over, Abram was met in the Valley of Sheveh by Melchizedek, the Priest/King of Salem (later called Jerusalem). He was the ruler of the Jebusites, a Canaanite people, and he is referred to in the Bible as "the priest of the most high God." The same order of high priest that Jesus is identified with in the book of Hebrews (chapter 7, verses 1-3). Melchizedek bought bread and wine with him when he came to bless Abram. From Abram, he received a tithe (10 percent) of all that he had. It is interesting to note the presence of these Christian symbols (bread, wine and tithe) in the time of Abram and their use by a Hamite priest.

After living among the Canaanites for 10 years, Abram was encouraged by Sarai to produce a child with Hagar, her Egyptian handmaid. Abram expressed no apprehensions about having sexual relations and producing a child with an Egyptian. From this relationship came Ishmael. At this time Abram was 86 years old. Ishmael is traditionally considered the ancestor of the Arabic people.

At the age of 99 Abram received a message from God changing his name to "Abraham" and his wife's name to "Sarah." Abraham was also given instructions to accept the African practice of circumcision. According to Herodotus "the Egyptians and Ethiopians are the only nations who practiced circumcision from the earliest times."[26]

According to the Bible, Abraham was given this practice as a covenant with God (Genesis 17:11). However, Diop believed Abraham's relationship with Hagar may have influenced the introduction of this practice. We learn

[26]Diop, *The African Origin of Civilization Myth or Reality*. pp. 135-136.

from the ancient geographer Strabo, who wrote in his *Geographical*: *"The Egyptians are especially careful in raising all their children and circumcise the boys and even the girls, a custom common to the Jews, a people originally from Egypt."*

The Dogon (of ancient Sudan) practiced circumcision and excision of their children to assure proper sexual inclination of the children during puberty. Like the Egyptians, they believed that the first god ("Amma" in Dogon and "Amen" in Egypt) was naturally androgynous and that this characteristic was passed on to new born babies. Therefore, the foreskin of the male penis was considered a female element, and the clitoris of the female vagina was considered a male element. The foreskin and clitoris were cut away to incline males toward full masculinity and females towards full femininity.[27] *(Book 17, chap.1, par.29)*

The genealogy of Abraham (in Figure 2) clearly shows that his descendants were not pure Hebrew. They were either Hebrew-Syrian, Hebrew-Egyptian or Hebrew-Canaanite. Even if Abraham and Sarah were pure Europeans (with blonde hair, blue eyes and white skin), their descendants would have lost their white appearance and culture through years of integration and miscegenation. Abraham had six children and five of them were Egyptians. Of his 21 grandchildren, 19 were Egyptians.

***Figure 2***
**The Genealogies of Abraham**

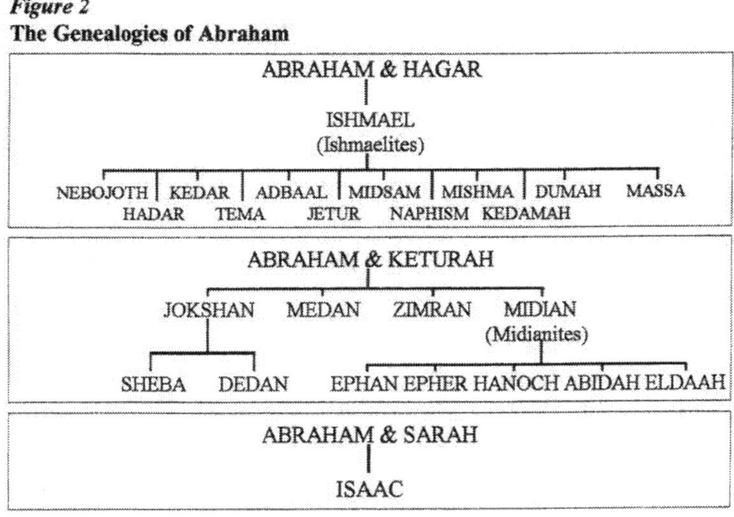


[27]Ibid., pp.136-137.

His son, Isaac, married a Syrian woman. The Syrians were depicted as Black people in ancient bas-reliefs and paintings. Isaac married Rebekah, the daughter of Bethuel "the Syrian." (Genesis 25:20) Abraham arranged their marriage, insisting that his son must marry a relative from his original home in the Mesopotamian region. Rebekah was Isaac's cousin and the great-granddaughter of Nahor, Abraham's brother. Abraham specifically stated that Isaac must not marry a Canaanite.

Isaac and Rebekah had twin sons, Esau and Jacob. Esau grieved his parents when he took three Hittite women as wives (Genesis 26:35). Nevertheless, Isaac intended to bless Esau as his heir, regardless of his Canaanite wives. However, this blessing went to Jacob, who conspired with Rebekah and tricked Isaac into giving the blessing to Jacob.

***Figure 3***
**The Genealogies of Isaac and Jacob**

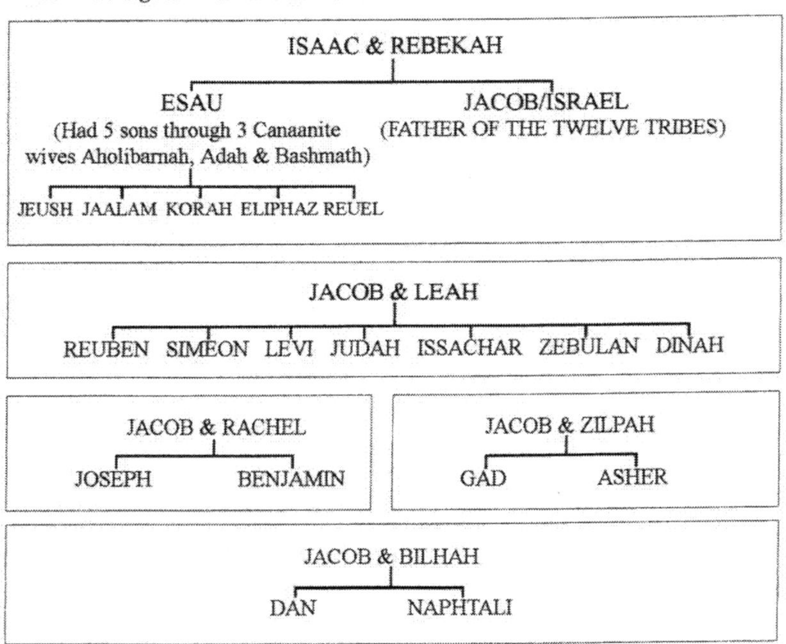


*Jacob's wives, Leah and Rachel, were Syrians; and their handmaids, Zilpah and Bilhah, were most likely Syrian or Egyptian. Therefore, the Children of Israel are predominantly of Syrian and/or Egyptian heritage.*

Jacob, like his father and grandfather, married within his family. Isaac sent him to Laban (Genesis 28), Rebekah's brother, to choose a wife of his daughters. Jacob arranged to serve Laban for seven years in exchange for taking Rachel, Laban's youngest daughter, as his wife. After the seven years Laban tricked him by giving him Leah, his oldest daughter, instead of Rachel. Jacob served him for seven more years to receive Rachel as his wife.

Rachel and Leah, like their aunt Rebekah, were Syrian. Both women had handmaids. Zilpah was a handmaid to Leah, and Bilhah was Rachel's handmaid. These women were most likely Egyptian or Syrian, considering Isaac's instructions for Jacob to not mix with any Canaanites. Like Sarah and Rebekah, Jacob's two wives experienced periods of barrenness. During these periods, their handmaids were used to produce children for Jacob.

A Syrian as depicted on the ceremonial walking stick of Tut-Ankh-Amon

Through these Syrian wives and their handmaids, Jacob gave birth to the 12 tribes of Israel. (Genesis 29-30) These were not white women. The biblical Syrians and Egyptians were Black people. The least that can be said about the children of Israel is they were a mixed Hebrew-Syrian and/or Hebrew-Egyptian people. However, this mixed heritage will end as the children of Israel become completely Egyptian, as is explained in the next chapter.

*Chapter 3*

# THE ISRAELITES BECOMING A KEMETIC PEOPLE

From the Bible we learn, in Chapter 37 of Genesis, that the jealousy and hatred felt by Joseph's older brothers was so great that they threw him into a pit and later sold him as a slave to some Ishmaelites. The Ishmaelites took Joseph to Egypt and sold him to Potipher, one of Pharaoh's officers and captain of the guard. After many tribulations and blessings, Joseph ultimately rose from being a prisoner to being a ruler in 13 years. At the age of 30 Joseph was given power to govern the resources of all the land of Egypt.

Pharaoh gave Joseph the name *Zephnathpaaneah*, which means "says the god, he will live." He was also given an Egyptian wife named Asenath. Together they had two sons, Manasseh and Ephraim. Joseph was later reunited with his family and forgave his brothers for the evil they did to him. Joseph made provisions for his family to live in Egypt, in the land of Goshen. According to Genesis 46:27, 70 members of the house of Jacob entered Egypt. The 70 included Jacob, his 12 sons, 51 grandsons, four great-grandsons, one daughter and one granddaughter. If we assume that all of his sons had one wife and half of his grandsons had wives, the total increases to 107 people.

Understanding the political atmosphere of Egypt is important to the argument that the children of Israel became an Egyptian people. It is believed that the Israelites entered Egypt around 1700 B.C.E., most likely after the Hyksos gained control of Egypt around 1730 B.C.E. According to Manetho, a 3rd Century Egyptian priest, the Hyksos were "invaders of obscure race...from regions of the east" and "men of ignoble birth."[28] Some historians believe that the Hyksos were white invaders from Asia. Therefore, the argument has been made that the children of Israel mixed with Asiatic Hyksos, instead of Black Egyptians.

---

[28]Martin Bernal, *Black Athena Vol.2*, New Brunswick, NJ: Rutgers University Press, 1991, p. 321 and Ivan Van Sertima and Runuko Rashidi, editors. *African Presence in Early Asia*, New Brunswick, NJ: Transaction Books, 1988, p. 190.

There are several historical facts that verify a relationship between the Hyksos and Israelites. However, little evidence exists to prove that they were white or Indo-European invaders from Asia. The children of Israel were shepherds. The name "Hyksos" is interpreted to mean "chieftains of the hill country" or "shepherd kings." If this name is an indication that the Hyksos were a rural and nomadic people, unlike the urban citizens of Egypt, they shared this lower cast status with the Israelites. According to Genesis 46:34, the Israelites were given living space in Goshen because they were shepherds and "every shepherd is an abomination unto the Egyptians." Martin Bernal writes, in *Black Athena*:

> *Apart from a general suggestion of a connection by the fact that the majority of Hyksos were, like the later Israelites, West Semitic speakers from Canaan, there are two specific reasons for supposing a more direct relationship. Firstly, there is the attestation in both Palestine and Lower Egypt of the name Ykb hr or Ykb as a Hyksos ruler in the late 18th Century. This name is remarkably similar to Jacob, Ya aqov. Jacob Israel was not only the eponym and the specific ancestor of Israel, he was also the patriarch who, according to tradition, led the Israelites into Egypt, Secondly, there is the archaeological evidence from the fact that by far the highest density of Hyksos scarabs (an ornament representing a scarab beetle) is to be found in the territory now known as the West Bank, which at the end of the Bronze Age was the Israelite heartland.*[29]

Considering the report of Manetho stating that the Hyksos were from "regions of the east," this may mean east in Egypt. Dr. Charles S. Finch, III, asserts, "It could more logically and plausibly be assumed that he [Manetho] was referring to the shepherds and nomads of Egypt's eastern desert...."[30] Finch also states that "the pastoral people living in Egypt's eastern desert were, in effect, Egyptian nationals who clung to their traditional way of life and were a constant source of turbulence and unrest." Classifying the Hyksos as Egyptian aboriginals may be complicated by their being a Semitic-speaking people. However, there were 16 Semitic languages spoken among the Ethiopians, two of which were Gheez and Amharic. What's more, it is

---

[29]Bernal, *Black Athena Vol.2*, p. 357.

[30]Van Sertima, *African Presence in Early Asia*, p. 191.

widely believed that Semitic languages grew out of Hamitic tongues. Bernal states that the "overwhelming majority of Hyksos in Egypt were Semitic-speaking and it is equally clear from names that, just as the material culture of the Hyksos at Tell el Dabaa became increasingly Egyptian in the 17th Century B.C.E., the Egyptian language reasserted itself in the face of the Semitic."[31]

The race of the Hyksos cannot be identified with absolute certainty. However, Manetho reports that an 18th Dynasty Egyptian inscription stated that the Hyksos capital contained "Semitic speakers of Syro Palestine" with "wanderers" or "foreigners in their midst."[32] This implies that the Hyksos included a mix of people from regions of Syria and Palestine, and people foreign to them. These "foreigners" and "wanderers" were most likely Indo-European people. According to Bernal, they were most likely non-Semitic speaking Hurrians or Indo-Iranian. Some historians, such as Eduard Meyer, have over-emphasized the "Indo-Aryan" presence among the Hyksos.[33] Yet, Bernal points out that the Hyksos language and culture was Syro-Palestinian.[34]

From the biblical perspective, no distinction is made in the Bible that identifies the Pharaoh as Hyksos. What's more, the Bible makes no mention of foreign rulers in Egypt when the Israelites entered with Jacob nor when they exited with Moses. Based on this omission, an argument can be made that the writers of the text considered the Hyksos to be convincing imitators of the Egyptian Pharaohs or actual Egyptians. These Hyksos Pharaohs of the Middle Kingdom (the 13th to the 17th Dynasties) lived as Egyptians. Gerald Massey, 19th Century lecturer and author of the *Book of Beginnings,* took the position that the Hyksos were not foreigners in Egypt.[35] The political and cultural structures of Egypt remained unchanged under Hyksos rule.

---

[31]Bernal, *Black Athena Vol.2*, p. 359.

[32]Ibid., p. 39.

[33]Eduard Meyer, *Reich und Kulter der Chetiter*: Berlin, 1914, p.58.

[34]Bernal, *Black Athena* Vol.2, p.41.

[35]Gerald Massey, *Book of Beginnings Vol.2*. London: Williams and Norgate, 1881, pp. 363-441.

Another interesting dimension to this issue is that of geographical boundaries. According to Allen H. Godbey, Hyksos power over Egypt was broken by Ahmose I in 1580 B.C.E. (before the exodus of the Israelites according to some sources). Well before Ahmose's victory, the "land of Egypt" extended geographically beyond the Sinai, north into Palestine.[36] Therefore, Godbey takes the position that the Israelites were not oppressed in Egypt, but in post-Hyksos dominated Palestine under Egyptian rule. This rule lasted four hundred years (until 1180 B.C.E.), which justifies the biblical 400 years of oppression of the Israelites (Genesis 15:13), plus 30 good years under Egyptian rule, while Joseph was in leadership.[37] From this perspective, regardless of when the exodus took place or where the Israelites were, the Israelites were under distinct Egyptian rule at the time of the exodus (as early as 1300 B.C.E., and as late as 1180 B.C.E.).

This is also the time frame (1200 B.C.E.) in which Israel historically emerges in Canaan. Biblical scholars have determined that the exodus story may represent the heritage of one segment of several tribes who united to comprise what came to be a common Israel, with common traditions, and common patriarchs.[38]

The biblical Israelites were subject to Egyptian rulers and lived among Egyptian people. These Israelites had Egyptian neighbors (Exodus 11:2 and 12:35). If there were other races and nations of people in Egypt, it is least likely that the Israelites would have intermixed with them. God did not put restrictions on their intermixing with Egyptians, as he did on their mixing with Canaanites. Neither God nor Jacob expressed any displeasure with Joseph having an Egyptian wife. In the 48th chapter of Genesis, Jacob proudly blessed Ephraim and Manasseh, the sons of Joseph and Asenath. These Egyptian men are the patriarchs of two of the Israelite tribes.

Around 1300 B.C.E., at the time of the exodus led by Moses, there were 603,550 men of fighting age (Numbers 1:46) among the Israelites. If we add

---

[36]Allen H. Godbey, *The Lost Tribes A Myth*, Durham, NC: Duke University Press, 1930, pp.692-694; and Colin McEvedy, *The Penguin Atlas of African History*, London: Penguin Books, 1980, pp.24-25.

[37]Godbey, *The Lost Tribes A Myth*, pp.694-695.

[38]Norman K. Gottwald, *The Hebrew Bible--A Social-Literary Introduction*, Philadelphia: Fortress Press, 1985, pp.143-144.

women, elderly women, elderly men and children, the number of those that Moses led from Egypt would be more than two million. This very conservative estimate is based on at least 300,000 of these men having one wife, two parents and two children. The exact total in this case would be 1.5 million women, elders and children. When the 603,550 men are added to this total, we have more than 2.1 million people being led by Moses. Furthermore, this number does not include the "mixed multitude" that exited with them, as reported in Exodus 12:38. A more liberal estimate may be more than 3 million people.

According to Genesis 15:13-16, the Israelites' oppressors would "afflict them four hundred years" and "in the fourth generation, they shall come hither again." The fulfillment of this prophesy is provided in Exodus 12:40, which states "Now the sojourning of the children of Israel, who dwelt in Egypt, was four hundred and thirty years." How could the Israelites grow from 107 people to at least 2.1 million people in 400 years? The only realistic way that this increase could have happened is by their intermixing and/or integrating with the Egyptians.

Furthermore, all of the generations of the Israelites (four generations according to Genesis 15:16) lived most of their lives in Egypt. More than 99.9 percent of the pre-exodus biblical Israelites were born in Egypt. The Israelites' ancestral ties began with Jacob Israel. His entire family migrated to Egypt and remained there for 430 years. Though they acknowledged their ethnic heritage as Israelites, they were Egyptian nationals.

The physical appearance of the Israelites was the same as the Egyptians. The earliest Israelites in Egypt were Hebrew Syrian and/or Hebrew-Egyptians.[39] After 430 years of living in the African climate and/or intermixing with the Egyptians, there was probably very little physical variance. Biblical proof for this position is established when the Midianite women refer to Moses as an "Egyptian" in Exodus 2:19. Midian was less than 150 miles from Egypt (and had probably been under Egyptian rule). The Midianites were descendants of Abraham and Keturah. These women knew what Egyptians looked like, and based on his appearance, they concluded that Moses was one.

---

[39]As reflected by the relationships identified in the genealogical diagram on page 22.

There are names used in the Bible that specifically indicate the race of the individual. According to Dr. Walter A. McCray, "an example of identifying a Black personal name is 'Kedar' (very Black), or 'Phinehas' (the Negro, or the Nubian)."[40] The Kedarites were descendants of Ishmael. There are three people identified by the name "Phinehas" in the Bible. The first one was the grandson of Aaron. If the grandchild is Black, it is likely that its parents and grandparents are Black.

The Bible clearly confirms that the Israelites were not naturally white people. In the 13th chapter of Leviticus laws are established for the priest regarding leprosy. This form of leprosy caused a physical mutation to occur in some cases. This mutation involved the skin developing "bright" spots, scabs, white hair and other symptoms. In Leviticus 13:11-13, the priest may declare the person "clean" if all of the skin is "turned white" from head to foot, providing that no raw flesh is visible. If the skin of a person with white spots became "dark" after seven days, they were declared clean. The turning of the skin to white must have caused fascination and fear among the Israelites and Egyptians. When God instructed Moses to show Pharaoh his leprous hand (Genesis 4:7), it was meant to be a threat to Pharaoh. God also used leprosy to punish Mariam, Moses' sister, as recorded in Numbers 12:10. She was turned white for seven days and put out of the camp until God restored her. It is fair to assume that they were dark-skinned people for whom whiteness would be uncommon.

The scriptures also confirm that the Israelites were familiar with Egyptian theology. In Exodus 3:14 God instructs Moses to tell the Israelites that "I Am hath sent me." One of the names of the supreme deity of Egypt was *Nuk Pu Nuk*, which means "I Am that I Am."[41] Jesus also refers to himself as "I Am" when he was challenged by certain Jews (John 8:58), for which they tried to stone him to death. The use of "I Am" as an identifier of who Moses was representing would make perfect sense to an Egyptian but is vaguely understood by modern Christians.

Similarly, the use of "Amen" in the Bible, and at the end of a Christian or Moslem prayer, has an Egyptian explanation. It is commonly defined as

---

[40]Walter Arthur McCray, *The Black Presence in the Bible, Vol.1*. Chicago: Black Light Fellowship, 1990, p. 20.

[41]Joseph Wheless, *Is It God's Word?*. New York: Alfred A. Knopf, 1926, p. 78.

meaning "verily" or "so let it be." However, in Revelations 3:14 Jesus is identified as "the Amen, the faithful and true witness, the beginning of the creation of God." The capitalizing of Amen identifies it as a proper noun. Therefore, it is more than a common exclamation, it is an identifier of someone in particular. In ancient Egyptian mythology, "Amen" or "Amon" is the name of one of the facets of the supreme God. Historian Anthony Browder states that Amen is "the personification of the sun after setting, when it was hidden from view in the underworld."[42] Amen is also the creator of the other facets of God, which are called "Netcherw." It was sacred tradition that every Egyptian ruler should be a son of Amen.[43] This is why many of the Pharaohs prefixed their names with "Amen" (e.g. Amenemhet and Amenhotep). Jean-Francois Champollion reported the Egyptian's belief that "Amon is the point of departure and the focal point of all divine essences." This is consistent with the theological status of Jesus Christ in Christianity.

According to Charles Finch, an etymological examination of important names and phrases used in the Bible reveals more Egyptian connections, shown in Figure 1 on page 32.[44]

The children of Israel also accepted Egyptian customs, starting with Joseph. Genesis 50:2 states that Joseph had his father's body embalmed. Embalming is a method of preserving a corpse that was started by the Egyptians and was not known among the Hebrews until Joseph had Jacob embalmed and placed in a coffin in Egypt. The practice was continued with the embalming of Joseph at his death. They also continued the practice of circumcision, an ancient Egyptian ritual.

In the 32nd chapter of Exodus the Israelites are called a "stiff necked people" (verse 9) by God, because they made a golden calf to worship while Moses was away from them. The worship of the calf was an Egyptian practice and was a form of sun worship. In Egyptian cosmogony there are many different deities and representations of the sun. In one Egyptian myth,

---

[42] Tony Browder, *Nile Valley Contributions to Civilization*. Washington, D.C.:The Institute of Karmic Guidance, 1992, p. 85.

[43] Will Durant, *The Story of Civilization, Part one: Our Oriental Heritage*. New York: Simon and Schuster, 1954, p. 153.

[44] Van Sertima, *African Presence in Early Asia*, pp. 193-196.

the sky is represented by a gigantic cow that gave birth to the sun. In this myth the sun is symbolized by a calf.[45] This form of worship was common to the Israelites according to Aaron from his statement to Moses: "You know the people, that they are set on mischief."

It is through Egypt that the children of Israel came into being. Some ancient traditions identify the Israelites as Egyptian or Ethiopian people. Tacitus, a 1st Century Roman historian, reported that "many assert that the Jews are an Ethiopian race."[46] Strabo identifies the Jews as "a people originally from Egypt.

***Figure 1***
**Egyptian and Hebrew words compared**[47]

**EGYPTIAN TERMS**
ATEM - The first god in the image of man
QEN - To beat, strike down or murder
NU-AKH - Flood waters that irrigate and fertilize the land
AB-REM - Father of the people
IB-RA-IM - Desire or wisdom of Ra's fire
YS-AKH - Place of burnt offering
YS-RA-IR - Place of Ra's Creation
YAH-WAH - The growing moon
JUHUDY - Name for the lunar deity Thoth
SET - An evil infertile deity

**HEBREW TERM**
ADAM - Man; the first man created by God.
QAYIN (Cain) -Spear; murdered his brother Abel
NUACH (Noah) - Rest; the builder of the ark
ABRAM - Exalted father
ABRAHAM - Father of a great multitude
YSAC (Isaac) - Laughter; the son Abraham was to offer as a sacrifice
ISRAEL - Having power with God
YAHWEH - Eternal one
JUHUDI (Judean) - Resident of Judea
SATAN - Adversary

---

[45]E.A. Wallis Budge, *The Book of The Dead*. Seraucus: University Books, Inc., 1960, pp. 132-133.

[46]Rudolphf R. Windsor, *The Valley of the Dry Bones*, Atlanta: Windsor's Golden Series, 1986, pp. 60,62 and Massey, *Book of Beginnings Vol.2*, pp. 428-433.

[47]Van Sertima, *African Presence in Early Asia*, pp. 193-196.

*Chapter 4*

# THE ISRAELITES SCATTERED AMONG THE NATIONS

Based on the information provided in the first three chapters, several historical truths can be added to popular Christian history and several misconceptions and lies can be put to rest. It is true that the Egyptian people of the Bible were Black; that the biblical Hebrews mixed with Black Semitic (Syrians) and Hamitic (Egyptians and Canaanites); and that the children of Israel were an Egyptian people. These truths put to rest long believed misconceptions and lies that upset historical continuity and balance of the biblical story. It is not true that Blackness was a curse imposed on Black people because of Cain's killing Abel or Canaan being cursed by Noah.[48] It is not true that the biblical Israelites were white. To be Black (or "people of color") was natural for the Israelites. Furthermore, it is not true that Adam, Noah, Abraham, Isaac, Jacob, or any of the Old Testament figures were white.

Before the children of Israel entered Egypt around 1706 B.C.E., they were a mix of Hebrew-Egyptian people. When they departed from Egypt around 1300 B.C.E., they were an Egyptian people that became a distinct nation called "Israel." In the 22nd chapter of Numbers, King Balak of Moab recognized the Israelites as a people "from Egypt." They may be compared to the British colonists who left, or were put out of, England and became Americans, South Africans or Australians. Though they all came from England, they became distinct nations of people based upon similar social conditions, religious beliefs, political struggles and geographical boundaries.

If the Israelites would have remained a pure nation by not intermixing with other nations, there would be no question of the ethnicity of Jesus and his New Testament contemporaries. However, according to the Bible, the Israelites often offended God by taking wives of other nations. The offense was not an issue of ethnic purity or racial pride. The offense involved the

---

[48]According to one etiology of Blackness as a curse, the "mark" God placed on Cain, in Genesis 4:15, was Blackness. Another more popular etiology asserts that Blackness and slavery were imposed on Black people when Noah cursed Canaan in Genesis 9:24-29.

worship of other gods that often occurred with intermixing.

The earliest Israelite laws instruct them to love the strangers among them and to treat them "as one born among" them.[49] Moses was married to a Midianite woman, yet this did not displease God. In the 25th chapter of Numbers, God is angered at the Israelites for worshiping the Moabite god Baal-Peor as a result of their intermixing with the Moabite women. For this offense, 24,000 men died from a plague. The plague was stopped by the actions of Aaron's grandson Phinehas (which can be interpreted as "the Nubian") when he killed an Israelite man and his Midianite companion. Because of his "zealous" action, Phinehas was blessed with a covenant of everlasting priesthood. (Numbers 25:6-13)

In the 31st chapter of Numbers, Israelite men were ordered to keep all of the Midianite girls who were virgins and to kill the women who were not virgins. These non-virgins were accused of causing the children of Israel to worship Baal-Peor and there was concern that they may continue to have this effect on the men of Israel. The number of virgin girls that the Israelite soldiers kept for themselves was 32,000. These girls probably became wives and concubines of the Israelites.

The following are scripture references detailing the Israelites intermixing with other nations and sometimes angering God by their idolatry.

***Examples of Biblical Miscegenation***

**Deuteronomy 23:7** - The Edomites are called a "brother" or "kin" to Israel; and the Israelites are instructed to not abhor the Edomites or the Egyptians and that their children may become members of Israel in their third generation.

**Judges 3:5-8** - The Israelites mixed with the Canaanites, Hittites, Amorites, Perizzites, Hivites and Jebusites.

**Judges 14:1-8** - Samson marries a Philistine woman.

---

[49] *The African Heritage Study Bible*, King James Version (The James C. Winston Publishing Company, Nashville, TN 1993) Leviticus 19:33-34 and Exodus 22:21.

**Ruth 1:3-4** - Elimelech and Naomi's sons marry Moabite women; one of her Moabite daughter in-laws was Ruth.

**Ruth 4:11-17** - Boaz and Ruth marry and give birth to Obed, the father of Jesse and grandfather of David. It is from this lineage that Jesus was born.

**II Samuel 11:3** - Bathsheba is the wife of Uriah the Hittite. David arranged for Uriah to be killed in order to take Bathsheba. This scripture shows that Hittites served in the Israelite army and that Hittites and Israelites intermixed.

**I King 3:1** - Solomon marries the daughter of an Egyptian Pharaoh.
**I King 11:1-4** - Solomon had 700 wives and 300 concubines. Among them were Moabites, Ammonites, Edomites, Zidonians and Hittites. God became angry with Solomon's idolatry.

**I King 16:31** - King Ahab of Israel married Jezebel, a Zidonian. He angered God with his idolatry.

**I Chronicles 2:3** - The sons of Judah were born of a Canaanite woman.

**I Chronicles 2:17** - Jether, David's brother-in-law, was an Ishmaelite.

**I Chronicles 2:35** -Sheshan, a leader of Judah, gives his daughter to Jarha, an Egyptian, to wed.

**Ezra 9:1,2** - Ezra reports that the people of Israel, the priest, and the Levites have taken wives of the Canaanites, Hittites, Perizzites, Jebusites, Ammonites, Moabites, Egyptians and Amorites. He states that the rulers and princes were the most notorious offenders.

**Ezra 10:2,18-44** - Ezra is informed that many of the Israelites have foreign wives and provides names of the fathers of those sons of Israel with strange wives.

**Nehemiah 13:23-31** - Reports that the Jews were married to women of Ashdod, Ammon and Moab, and that their children could not speak the "Jew's language."

**Esther 2-17** - Esther marries Ahasuerus, the king of Persia. As queen, she saved the lives of Jews when Haman plotted to kill them.

**Ezekiel 23** - The "word of the Lord" accused Samaria (Israelites) of intermixing with the Assyrians and Jerusalem (Judah) of mixing with the Chaldeans and Babylonians.

These scriptures identify specific people and nations that the Israelites/Jews mixed with. It is interesting to note that they only mixed with Hamitic and Semitic people. One possible exception is Esther's marriage to the king of Persia. The Persians are commonly considered Indo-European people. However, according to H.G. Wells, "There is a streak of very Negroid blood traceable in south Persia and some parts of India."[50] The following statement from historian Leo Hansberry further illuminates our understanding of Persian ethnicity:

> *The spread of the Aryan and the rise and spread of the Semitic and Mongolian peoples during the third and second millennium B.C.E. came into serious competition with the older Black population, and in the clashes and racial intermixture which followed, distinctive Black culture and ethnic traits were considerably dissipated. In some regions the original features were more definitely preserved; the Persian areas and its environs seems to have been one of these. In Persia the old Negroid element seems indeed to have been sufficiently powerful to maintain the overlordship of the land. For the Negritic strain is clearly evident in statuary depicting members of the royal family ruling in the second millennium B.C.E. Hundreds of years later, when Xerxes invaded Greece, the type was well represented in the Persian army.*[51]

The acknowledgment of Ahasuerus (the Persian king that took Esther as his wife) as the ruler of 127 provinces from India to Ethiopia confirms his close relationship with lands occupied by Black people south and west of Persia around 521 B.C.E. (Esther 1:1)

---

[50]H.G. Wells. *The Outline of History*. New York: The MacMillan Company, 1921, p. 109.

[51]Joseph E. Harris, editor. *Africa & Africans As Seen by Classical Writers*. Washington D.C.: Howard University Press, 1977, p. 52.

Around 940 B.C.E., Solomon was succeeded by his son Rehoboam as the king of Israel. Shortly after being made king, a civil conflict caused a revolution. The tribes of Judah and Benjamin (henceforth jointly called "Judah" or "Jews") were the only ones that remained loyal to Rehoboam. The other 10 tribes chose Jeroboam as the new king of Israel. The 12 tribes have never been reunited.

In 722 B.C.E. Israel was conquered by the Assyrians and ended as a national power. According to II Kings 17:6, the 10 tribes were carried away into Assyria, but some poorer Israelites were not taken. The Israelite cities left practically vacant after the expulsion were re-occupied by men from Babylon, Hamath and Sepharvaim. These people worshiped their own gods and were also trained in the worship of the God of Israel. Subsequently, the Israelites that were not taken and those foreigners trained in the worship of God came to be called "Samaritans."

The Samaritans were considered a mixed race by the Jews. It was bad enough that they were not pure Israelites and worshiped other gods. They also rejected Jerusalem as the center for true worship. David made Jerusalem the capital of Israel and Solomon built the temple there for the worship of God. The Samaritans chose Mt. Gerizim, near the city of Shechem, as their center of worship. They believed Mt. Gerizim to be the site where Abraham was to sacrifice Isaac. The Jews and Samaritans remained at odds into New Testament times.

In 586 B.C.E. Judah was conquered by Nebuchadnezzer, king of Babylon, who carried all of the Jews away to Babylon, except the "poorer sort of the people of the land" (II King 24:14). Persia conquered Babylon in 539 B.C.E. Cyrus II was ruler of Persia and Media. He ended the Babylonian captivity of the Jews after 70 years and allowed 42,000 Jews to return to Jerusalem to rebuild the temple. The Jews grew stronger under Persian rule. It took 20 years for them to rebuild the temple, which was completed in 515 B.C.E.

Confirming the popular belief that the New Testament Jews were white must involve proving that they and/or the nations that they intermixed with were white people. In the Old Testament, the word "white" is used 22 times in reference to skin color, all regarding leprosy.[52] The Hebrew word used in

---

[52]Leviticus 13 and Numbers 12:10. Leviticus 13:13 in particular, reports on leprosy covering the whole body, and the one afflicted being declared clean by the priest though that one's skin has "all turned white."

these scriptures is לָבָן (pronounced *laban*), which means to be or to become white.

In Song of Solomon 5:10, the lover (presumed to be Solomon) is called "white and ruddy." This use of white in the King James Version of the text does not refer to skin color, but rather to the lover as bright, radiant, or dazzling like a bright light. The allegorical nature of this scripture makes it difficult to conclude that Solomon had white skin. The Hebrew word used in this text is צַח pronounced *tsach*), which means dazzling, sunny or bright. A similar use of "whiter" and "ruddy" is found in Lamentations 4:7 about the Nazarites of Israel. Despite their being called "whiter than milk," this scripture also reports that their faces were "Blacker than a coal." This reference to Blackness seems to relate to a state of oppression.

Also in the Old Testament (Hebrew Bible) is the word "Black," which is used five times in reference to skin color. Of the five uses, three seem to imply Blackness of the Israelites as a state of oppression, famine or depression. For example, Job exclaimed, "My skin is Black (שָׁחַר, pronounced *shachar*) upon me and my bones are burned with heat."[53] The other two uses of "Black" are made by the Shulamite woman in the Song of Solomon. She proclaimed, "I am Black, but comely ....Look not upon me because I am Black (שְׁחוֹרָה, pronounced *shecharchoreth*), because the sun hath looked upon me; my mother's children were angry with me; they made me the keeper of the vineyard." It is clear that her Blackness is spoken of in connection with the oppression she experienced at the hands of her mother's children. The contemporary use of "Black" is quite different from these Old Testament applications. Yet their skin becoming deep Black implies melanin is present. A white person with a deep sunburn will be tan, red or brown, but certainly not Black.

Of the nations that the Israelites mixed with in the Old Testament, none of them were European whites. The Old Testament, which concludes with the book of Malachi around 400 B.C.E., gives no examples of white nations or individuals intermixing with the Israelites. The 400 years between the Bible books of Malachi and Matthew are called the "period of silence" or "intertestamental period" because the few existing writings from that period are not accepted as inspired or canonical. Professor of ancient history Morton Smith asserts that "cohabitation of Palestinian woman and Greek soldiers was

---

[53]*The African Heritage Study Bible*, Job 30:30.

frequent." He also reports that the Greek historian Hecataeus states, "Jewish intermixing with aliens was prevalent." This implies that the Jews intermixed with the Greeks without explicitly saying that the Palestinian women were Jews or that the aliens were Greeks.[54]

During these 400 years the Jews fell under Greek, Syrian and Roman domination. During the time of Nehemiah (444 B.C.E.) two different political movements existed among the Jews, which continued to impact Jewish history into New Testament times. The two movements involved one group of Jews that supported a separatist Jewish society and the other movement of Jews that wanted an assimilated Jewish society. The separatists advocated that Jews worship God (Yahweh) exclusively. They believed that the Gentiles (*ger* in Hebrew, which means "resident alien") could not become members of the Jewish people and they held very strict rules against intermixing. The assimilationists created the legal status of "proselyte" for the ger. This status allowed aliens to accept the Jewish laws and enjoy the rights it conferred.[55]

Ezra and Nehemiah spoke strongly against intermixing and agreed that the Gentiles could not be declared ritualistically "purified" or "pure." According to the purity law, reported in Haggai 2:10-14, to mix with nations that worshiped other gods or to touch items used in the worship of other gods made a Jew impure, the same as touching something dead would make a Jew impure.

However, Isaiah reported a new prophesy, which allowed aliens that followed Jewish laws to become pure as a natural Jew.[56] In Isaiah 49:6 and chapter 56 this prophesy is one of the earliest doctrines that allowed non-Israelites/Jews to become people of the God of Abraham, Isaac and Jacob. Before this belief, God (Yahweh) was viewed exclusively as the national god of the Israelites. This doctrine of assimilation prepared the way for Christianity by allowing non-Jews to receive the blessings and promises of God by accepting the Jewish laws. In New Testament teachings, these

---

[54]Morton Smith. *Palestinian Parties and Politics That Shaped the Old Testament*. London: SCM Press Ltd., 1987, p. 65.

[55]Ibid., p. 139.

[56]Norman K. Gottwald. *All The Kingdoms of the Earth*. New York: Harper & Row Publishers, 1964, p. 385 and Isaiah 56:1-8.

blessings are conferred by accepting Jesus as one's personal savior instead of accepting Jewish laws. This change from accepting Judaism to accepting Jesus was quite controversial and will be discussed in the 7th chapter.

It is likely that there were rare instances of intermixing between Jews and European whites, but not without complications. In addition to Jewish laws restricting intermixing, the Greeks also had laws against intermarriage. Language and cultural differences also served as barriers to intermixing. The separatist mindset continued into New Testament times. The Pharisees, which literally means "to separate," were a separatist party that originated from the earlier separatist movement. They wanted to make Jewish laity just as pure as the priest.[57] Greek, Syrian and Roman domination of Palestine will be examined in the next chapter, in connection with the political impact they had on New Testament times and the life of Jesus.

---

[57]J. Dwight Pentecost. *The Words and Works of Jesus Christ*. Grand Rapids: Academie Books of Zondervan Publishing House, 1981, pp. 542-553.

*Chapter 5*

# GREEK AND ROMAN RULE OVER ISRAEL

The popular canon of the Old Testament (Hebrew Bible) ends around 450 B.C.E. with the Jews under Persian rule. In 333 B.C.E. Palestine fell under Greek rule through the leadership of Alexander the Great, who was met in Jerusalem by a peaceful procession of Jews led by the High Priest to surrender to Greek authority.[58]

He conquered Egypt in 332 B.C.E. and founded the city of Alexandria. At the invitation of Alexander, a large colony of Jews migrated to Alexandria and later grew to be the largest home of Jews outside of Palestine. Aside from Jews, Alexandrian citizenry also included many Greeks, Persians, Syrians and Egyptians.[59]

Despite Greek and Roman rule, the Palestinian region maintained its population of Semitic and Hamitic people. According to Strabo, at the end of the 1st Century the territory around Jerusalem was "inhabited in general, as is each place in particular, by mixed stocks of people from Egyptian [by which he means Jewish] and Arabian and Phoenician tribes; such, moreover, are those who occupy Galilee and Jericho and Philadelphia and Samaria."[60]

In 323 B.C.E. Alexander died and the lands conquered by him were divided among his generals. General Ptolemy I Sotar gained control of Egypt and Palestine. In addition to having a museum built in Alexandria, he is well known for using Egyptian ideologies to produce a national deity called "Serapis." Ptolemy I declared that he was given a revelation in a dream, which revealed to him the image of Serapis. A statue was immediately

---

[58]J. Dwight Pentecost. *The Words and Works of Jesus Christ*. Grand Rapids: Academie Books of Zondervan Publishing House, 1981, p. 530.

[59]Max Radin. *The Jews Among the Greeks and Romans*. Philadelphia: Jewish Publication Society of America, 1915, p. 92.

[60]Morton Smith. *Palestinian Parties and Politics that Shaped the Old Testament*. London: SCM Press LTD, 1987. p. 65.

constructed. The resulting image is similar to the popular white portrayal of Jesus of modern times. Some historians argue that "this icon/image was a predecessor of the Jesus Christ Image."[61] The worship of Serapis gained much support in Greece, Asia Minor, Sicily and Rome. It was not well received by the Egyptians and resisted by the monotheistic Jews and Persians.

Ptolemy II Philadelphus succeeded his father in 285 B.C.E. and was considered a friend to the Jews. Many more Jews moved to Egypt during his rule. Two of his greatest accomplishments were the founding of the Library of Alexandria and having the Hebrew scriptures translated into Greek, the common language of the time.

According to tradition, it took 72 Jewish scholars 72 days to produce this Greek version of the *Pentateuch*, the Hebrew version of the first five books. The Letter of Aristeas, written by a courier of Ptolemy II to his brother, reports that six leading scholars were chosen from each tribe. He also describes the conflicts that existed between the Hellenic Jews of Alexandria and the Hebraic Jews of Palestine. It took more than 200 years to translate all of the Hebrew writings. This Greek version of the Old Testament is called the *Septuagint*, which means "seventy." Biblical scholar Dr. Neil R. Lightfoot says, "It is believed that the version was completed at Alexandria, but probably by Alexandrian rather than Palestinian Jews."[62] Scriptures from the Septuagint were often quoted by Jesus and other New Testament figures.

In 204 B.C.E. the Seleucidae rulers of Syria gained control of Palestine. Seleucus I Nicator, another one of Alexander's generals, became the first ruler of this dynasty in 323 B.C.E. The fifth successor of the dynasty, Antiochus IV Epiphanes, seized control of Palestine from the Ptolemies. At this time the land was divided into five provinces. These provinces were Judea, Samaria, Galilee, Trachonitis and Perea. Antiochus IV greatly persecuted the Jews. His contemporaries considered him to be "a madman" and "unqualifiedly demented." He had 40,000 Jews put to death, sold many others into slavery and profaned the Temple in Jerusalem by offering a pig on

---

[61]Jill Kamil. *Coptic Egypt*. Cairo: The American University in Cairo Press, 1987, p. 20.

[62]Neil R. Lightfoot. *How We Got the Bible*. Grand Rapids: Baker Book House, 1963, p. 73 and Stephen L. Harris. *Understanding the Bible*. Palo Alto, CA: Mayfield Publishing Company, 1980, pp. 191-192.

its altar. Further persecution included restricting synagogue services, the re-dedication of the Jerusalem Temple to the god Zeus, declaring circumcision a capital offense and declaring observance of the Sabbath an act of treason.[63]

The oppressed Jews responded with an insurrection led by a priest named Mattathias. He gained fame by killing two of Antiochus' commissioners and an apostate Jew who was worshiping at an idol altar. Despite being up in age, he led an army into the mountains of Judea and conducted guerilla warfare against the forces of Antiochus IV. Mattathias fought until his death and was succeeded by Judas, one of his five sons. Judas led his inferior Jewish forces to victory in three decisive battles against the forces of Antiochus IV. The Seleucidae ruler died of disease while making new plans to increase persecution of the Jews.

Judas was given the name Maccabaeus, meaning "the hammerer," because of his successful leadership in war. Judas Maccabaeus became the Priest-King of Judea in 163 B.C.E. and the Maccabees' Hasmonian dynasty (named after Hasmon, an ancestor of Mattathias) maintained independent rule in Palestine until a civil war erupted in Judea. The conflict resulted from disputed claims between Aristobulus II and John Hyrcanus II, both decendants of Mattathias. The claims were submitted for arbitration to Pompey, a Roman general. Pompey favored the claim of Hyrcanus II. Aristobulus II continued to dispute the decision and was defeated in battle by Pompey, who took control of Jerusalem and appointed Hyrcanus II ethnarch (provincial governor) of Palestine in 63 B.C.E.

A Jewish relationship with the Romans was first established through a treaty of friendship initiated by Simon, the third son of Mattathias and the fourth Priest-King of the Hasmonian dynasty. This treaty was renewed by Hyrcanus II. The title of "ethnarch" emphasizes the fact that Judea then became one of many provinces of the Roman empire.[64] While under Roman rule, the Jews were given full religious rights and political liberty, but they were made to pay a yearly tribute.

Around 47 B.C.E. Roman Emperor Julius Caesar appointed Hyrcanus II as the King of Judea and appointed Antipater, a wealthy Idumean (Edomite) officer, its procurator. He also appointed Herod, Antipater's son, as governor of Galilee. Herod grew in power and later married Mariamne, the

---

[63]Radin, *The Jews Among the Greeks and Romans*, pp. 136,143.

[64]Harris, *Understanding the Bible*, p. 213.

granddaughter of Hyrcanus II. Political conflicts in Rome led to the assassination of Julius Caesar. The conspirators in the assassination were forced into exile by Mark Antony, who gained almost complete control of the Roman empire. Around 40 B.C.E. Antony appointed Herod as the King of Judea. It was this Herod that the New Testament identifies as having Jewish babies put to death out of fear that the long-awaited Messiah was born.

During Greek and Roman rule many Jews accepted some elements of the Hellenistic culture (Greek style of dress, language, names and ideas). Hellenistic Jews were commonly found in Alexandria and the Galilee region of Palestine, but not in Judea. The Judeans maintained a strong commitment to Jewish ideas and customs. After years of subjugation to other nations, the Hebrew language was no longer common to the Jews. After the Babylonian exile, most of them spoke *Aramaic.* It was the language of the Syrians (or Aramites) that was spoken by the Babylonians after 1000 B.C.E. and was also the official language of the Persian Empire after 500 B.C.E. In the 1st Century C.E. some Jews spoke *Koine*, a tongue that resulted from the fusion of classical Greek and the commercial vernacular of Near Eastern people. The entire New Testament was written in Koine.[65]

There were five principle sects or political parties among the New Testament Jews. These five parties were the Pharisees, Sadducees, Essenes, Zealots and Herodians. The Pharisees (which means "to separate") strongly resisted foreign influence and observed the Jewish laws with legalistic fervor. They also believed in an afterlife and resurrection.

The Sadducees were composed of Jewish aristocrats and held many important positions on the Sanhedrin, which served as the supreme judicial council of the Jews. It was the Sanhedrin that found Jesus guilty of blasphemy, which led to his crucifixion. The Sadducees were ultraconservative and placed much emphasis on politics and none on religion.

The Essenes were a sect that lived an isolated communal life west of the Dead Sea. Their lives consisted of reading the scriptures, having worship services and sometimes engaging in a baptism ritual. The Essenes are not mentioned in the Bible but, they were a major sect during New Testament times.

The Zealots were the revolutionary Jews who wanted to gain their independence through war with Rome. Judas Iscariot, the betrayer of Jesus,

---

[65]Ibid., p. 7.

was a member of this group.

The Herodians were supporters of the government of Herod. They believed that this foreign (Idumean) rule provided the best hope for protection of their lives and property.[66]

Popular among the Jews was the anticipation of the "Expected One" who would come to deliver them from their foreign rulers. They anticipated that this king would lead them in physical battle against the foreign rulers, restore the Temple and reunify the 12 tribes of Israel. The book of Daniel foretold of the "Ancient of Days" that would give "glory and kingship" to "one like a Son of Man." It was expected that he would be a "Son (descendant) of David." Millions of people believe that Jesus was, and is, this "Expected One" and has been given the title "Messiah" or "Christ," both of which mean "anointed one."

---

[66]Pentecost, *The Words and Works of Jesus Christ*, p. 542.

*Chapter 6*

# THE BIBLICAL AND HISTORICAL JESUS

The Apostles' Creed states that Jesus is the Son of God, "who was born of Mary the Virgin, was crucified under Pontius Pilate, on the third day rose from the dead, ascended into Heaven, sits at the right hand of the Father, from which he comes to judge the living and the dead."[67]

It is believed that Jesus was born around 4 B.C.E., probably in March or April, and was put to death April 4, 33 C.E.[68] Most people assume the story of Jesus is well documented biblically and historically. This may or may not be true, based on what one is willing to accept as credible historical sources.

From a biblical perspective, many Bible scholars have doubts about who the authors of the New Testament books were and when the books (or letters) were written. Most scholars agree that the Book of Mark is the first of the Gospels written, and was followed by Matthew, Luke and John. The later writers most likely used the book of Mark and added the stories of Jesus' birth. Since the beginning of Christianity, there have been controversies about which books should be canonized (accepted as truly God-inspired Christian literature) and which ones lack credibility. In fact, the books of Peter, James, Jude, Hebrews and Revelation were all heavily disputed by some early Christians.[69]

Some of the apostles of Jesus (the 12 men trained and commissioned by Jesus personally) doubted the authenticity of Paul's conversion and his authority as an apostle, an issue still debated by some. There are many Christian ministers today who reject his authority. These and other matters

---

[67]Kenneth Scott Latourette. *A History of Christianity Vol.I.* New York: Harper & Row Publishers, 1975, p. 135.

[68]J. Dwight Pentecost. *The Words and Works of Jesus Christ.* Grand Rapids: Academie Books of Zondervan Publishing House, 1981, pp. 56-57,572.

[69]Stephen L. Harris. *Understanding The Bible*. Palo Alto: Mayfield Publishing Company, 1980, p. 19.

produce some difficulty in developing historical certainty regarding the life of Jesus, and cause complications in developing religious doctrines for Christians to live by.

From a historical perspective, there is limited evidence (beyond the Biblical) from the time Jesus lived to verify the Gospel accounts of his life. The Bible and non-canonical documents that support the stories of Jesus' life are often dismissed by critics as subjective Christian propaganda and myth. The lack of evidence current to the time of Jesus does not mean that the Gospels are not credible, or that he never existed. It is understandable that the Christian writers developed a better understanding of the ministry and personal history of Jesus after the time of his death and resurrection.

There also exists non-Christian references to the existence of Jesus. The 1st Century Roman historian Tacitus reported that a man called *Christus* was executed under Tiberius and Pontius Pilate. The report about Jesus by Josephus is given in his *The Antiquities of the Jews*, though not preserved in its original form.[70]

Gerald Massey rejects these sources as "forgeries" and argues that the lack of "contemporary testimony or recognition" is due to the biblical Jesus being a mythical figure based on a 1st Century B.C.E. man named Jehoshua ben Pandira, as recorded in the Talmud. Jehoshua (or Yehoshua) is the original Aramaic for the more popular Greek version of the name "Jesus." The Talmud reports that Jehoshua was trained in Egypt, performed many miracles and was put to death as a sorcerer.[71]

It took many years for the biblical image of Jesus to crystalize. The nature of Christ was still being disputed by church leaders well into the 5th Century B.C.E. and the development of the many different Christian denominations resulted from varying interpretations.

The acknowledgment of Jesus as "Christ" is an important element of the Christian theology. The title "Christ" is derived from the Greek term Χριστ ς (*Christos*), which means the anointed. It is equivalent to the Hebrew מָשׁח (*mashiackh*), from which the word "messiah" is derived. There is also a belief that the term "Christ" has some affinity to the Egyptian term *KRST* (or

---

[70]Helmut Koester. *History and Literature of Early Christianity Vol.2*. New York: Walter De Gruyter, 1987, p. 14 and Harris, *Understanding the Bible*, p. 220.

[71]Gerald Massey. *The Historical Jesus and The Mythical Christ*. Brooklyn: A&B Books Publishing, 1992, pp. 188-191.

*karast*), which refers to the mummification process of embalming a corpse, perfuming it and standing it upright. The common Hebrew concept of anointing involved the belief that a person anointed with certain oils gained superior or supernatural powers. According to J.A. Rogers, "Christ" comes from the Indian term *Krishna* or *Chrishna*, meaning "The Black One."[72]

The pre-Christian era Jewish anticipation of an "Expected One" was expressed in the post-Christian era as the "Christ." The recognition of Jesus as Christ did not come easy and the establishing of Christianity as a religion independent of Judaism took many years.

It is difficult to establish biblical and historical consensus about the life of Jesus. The issue of how early Christians depicted him physically is just as complicated and probably more controversial.

Since the 2nd Century, there have been physical depictions made of Jesus. The Bible gives no description of him. In the book of Isaiah (Chapter 53, Verse 2) a prophesy is given that is accepted as being about Jesus, which says "he has no form or comeliness; and when we shall see him, there is no beauty that we should desire him." In Revelations 1:15 and Daniel 7:9 he is described, metaphorically, as having hair like wool and feet like burned brass.

In the 4th Century one depiction of Jesus became quite popular. This image was based on the *Letter of Lentulus*, supposedly written during the time Jesus lived by a Roman official named Lentulus. The letter lacks credibility and was most likely a forgery. Lentulus (whose existence is questionable) was supposedly Pontius Pilate's superior and was believed to have written a report to Tiberius Caesar, including a warrant for the arrest of Jesus that provided this physical description:

> *At this time there appeared and is still living a man, if indeed he can be called a man at all, of great powers named the Christ, who is called Jesus. The people term him the prophet of truth; his disciples call him Son of God, who wakens the dead and heals the sick, a man of erect stature, of medium height, fifteen and a half fist high, of temperate and estimable appearance, with a manner inspiring of respect, nut-brown hair which is smooth to the ears and from the ears downward shaped in gentle locks and flowing down over the shoulders in ample curls, parted in the middle after the manner of*

---

[72]J.A. Rogers. *Sex and Race Vol.1*. St. Petersburg: Helga M. Rodgers, 1967, p. 265.

*the Nazarenes, with an even and clear brow, a face without spot or wrinkles, and of healthy color. Nose and mouth are flawless; he wears a luxuriant beard of the color of his hair. He has a simple and mature gaze, large, blue-grey eyes that are uncommonly varied in expressiveness, fearsome when he scolds and gentle and affectionate when he admonishes. He is gravely cheerful, weeps often, but has never been seen to laugh. In figure he is upright and straight. His hands and arms are well shaped. In conversation he is grave, mild and modest, so that the word of the prophet concerning the 'fairest of the sons of men' (Psalms 45:2) can be applied to him.*[73]

This letter lacks credibility because of its blatant flattery of Jesus, uncommon for a Roman official. Its identification of Jesus as the Christ, Son of God and Prophet of truth were all ascribed to him after his crucifixion. The use of a scriptural reference further proves that it was written by a Christian supporter of Jesus and not a Roman official who wanted to arrest him.

In 705 C.E., during the second rule of the Roman Emperor Justinian II, a gold coin was minted that had Justinian and Tiberius on one side and Jesus on the other. The image of Jesus on this coin is of a man with an afro, facial hair of crisp curls, thick lips and a full nose. This image replaced a more European image that appeared on an earlier coin.[74]

*Provided courtesy of Dr. Charles Finch, III.*

Paintings of Jesus from the 2nd and 3rd Centuries C.E. are found in the Catacomb of Domitilla. One painting shows a profile of a man with a thin nose, thin lips, very dark skin and black hair. Another painting, called "The Good Shepherd," shows a very dark-skinned young man with an afro-like

---

[73]Ernst Benz. *The Eastern Orthodox Church*. Garden City: Anchor Books of Doubleday & Company, Inc., 1963, pp.12-13.

[74]Daud Malik Watts. *The Black Presence in the Land of the Bible*. Washington, D.C.: Afro Vision, Inc., 1990, pp. 22-23.

hair style.[75]

There are no known portrayals of Jesus from the 1st Century C.E. and very few assigned to the 2nd Century. Jesus did not become a hero to European people until more than 300 years after he lived. They had no reason to honor him with portraits and statues. The Christians were basically considered enemies of Rome until the 4th Century C.E. when, under the rule of Constantine, the Edict of Milan ended persecution of the Christians. After the reign of Constantine, Christianity was made the official religion of the Roman empire.

Unlike today, they had no cameras, video tapes or computers to record and maintain an accurate image of Jesus or his contemporaries. Under Roman persecution, the destruction of Christian literature and symbols often occurred. This may account for the lack of images of Jesus from Christian communities of the first 300 years of the religion. It is unwise to expect a former oppressor to depict the national heroes of its former enemy accurately. The Romans could not defeat the Christians, so they absorbed them into Roman culture in the 4th Century. This assimilation produced a synthesized version of the religion and synthesized images to represent the religion. However, there were a few images produced in Rome that depict Jesus as a Black man, such as the 7th Century gold coin shown on page 63.

Despite the lack of early images, the portrayals of Jesus and Mary, popularly known as the "Black Madonna and Child," remain as positive proof that they were perceived as Black people. In 1125 C.E. Rupert the Benedictine stated that paintings of Mary, common to his time, show her as "dark" and "Black."[76] Today, there may be as many as 600 Black Madonnas, mostly in Europe.

In the 16th Century C.E. there were 190 known Black Madonnas in France and today there may be as many as 300 there. According to William Mosley, author of *What Color Was Jesus?* "Hundreds of thousands make the annual pilgrimage to the Shrine of the Black Madonna at Alt-Otting in West Germany." He also states that "Many believe that through contact with these images one can be healed of sickness and diseases, and there have been many

---

[75]Joan Comay and Ronald Brownrigg. *Who's Who in the Bible*. New York: Bonanza Books, 1980, pp. 155,179.

[76]John L. Johnson. *The Black Biblical Heritage*. Nashville: Winston-Derek Publishers, Inc., 1993, p. 203.

published reports to that affect. *The Black Virgin of Kazan*, also called 'the miracle Ikon of Holy Russia,' is noted for the alleged miracles it has performed."[77]

The fact that Jesus was a 1st Century Jew supports the belief that he was a Black man. In his family lineage are found Hamite women (Tamar, Rahab and Bathsheba). He was of the tribe of Judah, considered a rabbi (teacher) by his contemporaries and allowed to teach in the synagogue. This respect and authority would not have been given to him if he were not perceived as a pure Jew.

In 2002 *Popular Mechanics* magazine raised the ire of many of its readers by publishing a cover story entitled "The Real Face of Jesus." By using modern techniques in forensic anthropology, researcher A. Midori Albert was able to construct an image of what a normal Galilean Semite of Jesus time would look like. The resulting image, which appears on the cover of the December 2002 edition of the magazine, depicts Jesus as a dark-skinned man with brown eyes, Black curly/woolish hair, mustache and beard, a broad nose and thick lips.[78]

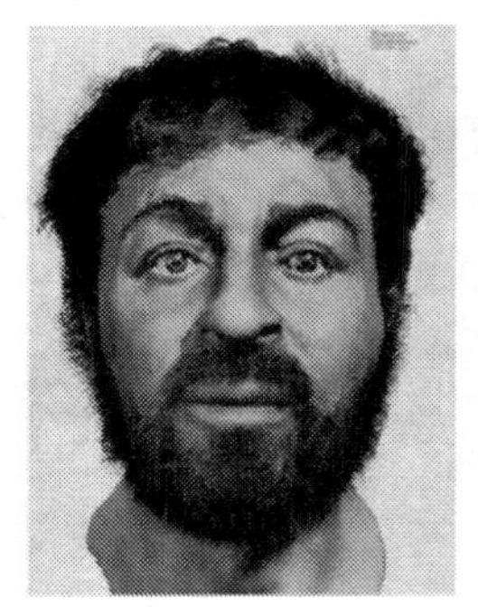

Traditions about Jesus' supposed marriage to Mary Magdalene have also given perspective to the concept of Jesus' ethnicity. Mary Magdalene is certainly a somewhat enigmatic biblical personality. Questions loom regarding her character, identity and ethnicity. It is possible that she was an African woman from Magdala in Ethiopia.[79] According to a popular legend from the southern coast of France, in 42 C.E. several Christians arrived in a boat with no oars on the Mediterranean coast of Gaul in order to escape

---

[77]Watts, *The Black Presence in the Land of the Bible*, p. 18 and William Mosley. *What Color Was Jesus*. Chicago: African American Images, 1987, p. 20.

[78]*Popular Mechanics*, "Real Face of Jesus" by Mike Fillon, December 2002

[79]Lynn Picknett. *Mary Magdalene: Christianity's Hidden Goddess.* New York: Carroll & Graf Pub, 2003

Christian persecution. Among the voyagers was Mary Magdalene and a young girl who was presented as her servant girl but is purported to be Jesus' and Mary Magdalene's daughter. The child is identified as "Sarah the Egyptian," or "*Sarah la Kali*," which literally means "Black Sarah." Though it cannot be proven that she was the daughter of Mary Magdalene (or Jesus), it is interesting to note that the one person who is traditionally or historically referred to as the offspring of Jesus is also Black.

There is no sin in seeing Jesus as a Black man. Many people say that "it does not matter what color he was," yet they refuse to replace their "white Jesus" image with a Black one. Some people choose to use no image, but this will not erase the white image embedded in their minds.

The biblical Jesus was a Black man. As a carpenter he was physically strong. He lived part of his life with no father. He came from Nazareth, a town in the Galilee region of Palestine where the people had the reputation of being of "passionate and lawless character."[80] He was considered a threat by the established political and religious leaders. He was a revolutionary who chose to change the world with a sword of truth. He was tried as a criminal and put to death.

Many people would benefit from knowing this perspective of Jesus. Like Jesus, many people work as laborers; are fatherless; live in communities where the people have the perceived reputation of being lawless; are considered a threat to society; and are tried as criminals and put in prison to die. It may not matter to some people what color Jesus was, but it may make the difference to those who have rejected the Gospel as "the white man's religion."

---

[80]Pentecost, *The Words and Works of Jesus Christ*, p. 521.

*Chapter 7*

# JESUS' DISCIPLES AND APOSTLES

The biblical Jews of Palestine were a people subject to factionalism, who were split into several different religious and political sects. The most influential sects were the Pharisees, Sadducees, Essenes, Zealots and Herodians (described in Chapter 5). The movement headed by Jesus was not considered a major sect until the end of his life.

The salvific story of Jesus is presented as the central theme of the New Testament. The Bible offers reports on the ministry of Jesus from which some assume it "spread like wild fire" immediately following the resurrection. However, it took almost 500 years for the impact of the ministry of Jesus to spread slowly and grow as a world power. Responsible for initiating this growth process were the disciples and apostles of Jesus. The word "disciple" represents the Greek word μαθητε ω (*matheteuo*), which means to become a pupil or learner. According to J. Dwight Pentecost, author of *The Words and Works of Jesus Christ*, being a disciple "does not suggest that one accepts the word of a teacher, only that he will listen." The word "apostle" comes from the Greek word ἀπόστολος (*apostolos*), which means messenger or "he that is sent." The apostles held the special status of being those personally sent by Jesus and endowed with the authority given to him by God.

It is fair to conclude that the apostles and disciples were Black Jews. There is no reason to assume that they were white, as they are popularly portrayed. There may have been a few white Gentiles who became proselytes and lived according to Jewish laws. There were some instances of intermixing by a few Hellenized Jews (Eunice is one example, Acts 16:1). However, they would be treated like the Samaritans, with scorn if they worshiped any other Gods.

The Romans looked upon intermixing with displeasure and had laws against intermarriage, as did the Greeks. Peter speaks of these laws in Acts 10:28, where he states, "It is an unlawful thing for a man that is a Jew to keep company or come unto one of another nation." It is important to understand that laws and customs restricting intermixing among the Jews, Greeks and Romans were not based on race. In the 4th Century C.E., Constantine said,

"Every animal is prompted by nature to seek a mate among the animal of his own species and as the human species is divided into various tribes by the distinction of language, religion, and manners, a just regard to the purity of descent preserves the harmony of public and private life."[81] This statement says nothing about race and the present type of racism didn't exist in the Roman Empire. Septimus Severus, an African, was the Emperor of Rome from 193 to 211 C.E. and there were many different races of people among the Roman citizenry. The Apostle Paul was a Roman citizen, though he was a Jew.[82]

A Gentile could become a Jew by accepting Jewish laws, which included the worship of God (Yahweh) only and being circumcised. This was a price that most Gentiles would not pay. The difficulty in properly converting Gentiles was expressed by Jesus in the New Testament (Matthew 23:15), where he states, "Woe unto the scribes and Pharisees, hypocrites! For you cross sea and land to make one proselyte (converted Gentile), and when he is made, you make him twice as much the child of hell than you are." Undoubtedly, the scribes and Pharisees did not properly convert some Gentiles in Jesus' lifetime.

Purity was a major issue for the Jews of Palestine because they were the last stronghold of the worship of God (Yahweh) exclusively and the hope for the re-establishment of Israel. The teachings of Jesus seemed to represent the aspirations of many staunch Jews. He attracted many students with his teachings.

The "disciples of Jesus," when stated in the New Testament Gospels, generally refers to the 12 Apostles. These 12 men were symbolic of the 12 tribes of Israel. Most of them were unlearned men of lower social status. Jesus had many more disciples, probably thousands. John, one of the 12, reported on a man casting out demons in the name of Jesus, though the man did not "follow" with them. Many disciples stopped following Jesus because of his unorthodox teachings (John 6:60-66) and "all the disciples forsook him" when he was arrested and taken to be crucified (Matthew 26:56). It was customary for one Jewish prisoner to be released during the Passover season.

---

[81]J.A. Rogers. *Sex and Race, Vol.III*. St. Petersburg, FL: Helga M. Rogers, 1944, p. 5.

[82]J.C. deGraft-Johnson. *African Glory*. Baltimore: Black Classic Press, 1986, p. 30.

Jesus had become so unpopular that the Jews demanded that he be crucified for blasphemy and chose to release a murdering thief named Barabbas.

The events recorded in the Bible following the trial of Jesus provide the foundation for Christian theology. These events begin with the death of Jesus on the cross. On the third day he was resurrected from the dead. He appeared before the disciples and many other people several times over a 40-day period. He commissioned the disciples to "go and make disciples of all nations" (Matthew 28:19). He ascended into the sky from the Mount of Olives. Two angels appeared, stating that Jesus would return "in like manner as you have seen him go into heaven" (Acts 1:11).

On the day of Pentecost (an annual feast) in Jerusalem, 120 followers of Jesus received the "Holy Spirit" (also called the Comforter) while praying in the "Upper Room." The spirit gave them the ability to speak the languages of other people. There were Jews from many nations in Jerusalem for the feast and "amazed and astonished, they asked 'Are not all these who are speaking Galileans?'" (Acts 2:5-7). This scripture provides the nationalities of these Jews as Parthians, Medes, Elamites, Mesopotamians, Judeans, Cappadocians, Phrygians, Pamphylians, Egyptians, Libyans, Cretes and Arabians. These were all Near East Asian and African people. It also states that there were "strangers of Rome" present who were Jews and proselytes. Rome is the only European nation mentioned. Identifying them as "strangers" is a clear indication that they were not considered familiar Jews like the Near East Asian and African Jews.

The spread of Christianity during the 1st Century C.E. was led by the Apostles. Eleven of them were personally chosen by Jesus. Their names were Simon Peter, Andrew, James (son of Zebedee), John, Philip, Bartholomew, Thomas, Matthew, James (son of Alphaeus), Thaddaeus (or Judas, son of James) and Simon the Zealot. The apostles later chose Matthias, to replace Judas Iscariot, who hung himself after betraying Jesus.

Jesus told these men, "...and you will be my witnesses in Jerusalem, in all Judea and Samaria, and to the ends of the earth" (Acts 1:8). The Bible reports that the followers of Jesus in Antioch, Syria were called Χριστιαν ς (*Christianos* or Christians)." This word was used only once in the Bible, in Acts 11:26.

From a theological perspective, they were empowered with the Holy Spirit to spread the Gospel (good news) of Jesus. This Gospel of Jesus involved teaching that Jesus was the "Expected One" and "Messiah" of the Jews and that he established a spiritual Kingdom of God where the believers would enjoy eternal fellowship with God. They taught that Jesus, through his death and resurrection, became the sacrifice and symbol of true life and victory over death and sin. They taught that all people would be judged by Jesus on "Judgement Day" and through belief in Jesus as their Savior they would avoid the punishment of hell's fires.

The Old Testament laws, given through Moses, were therefore supplanted by a New Testament gospel given through Jesus. The word testament means "covenant." The old covenant involved the Israelites observance of laws given to Moses by God. By strict observance of these laws, the Israelites enjoyed the blessings and favor of being the "Chosen People" of God (Yahweh) whose sacrificial offerings led to forgiven for their sins. The new covenant involved a personal commitment to God through belief in Jesus. Through the belief and acceptance of the salvation offered through Jesus as the sacrifice for sins, an individual received the Holy Spirit and forgiveness for their sins.

Before the new covenant, God (Yahweh) was the primary god of Israel, and they were his people. Likewise, Amen was the primary god of Upper (southern) Egypt, and Baal was the primary god of the Canaanites. After the new covenant, God was presented as the only true God and Creator of the world, rather than a mere national deity. Jesus is presented as a sort of personal deity, through which an individual became a "child of God." Therefore, an individual relationship with God became dependent upon their personal relationship with Jesus, rather than there being a Jew or by only observing Jewish laws.

It was this belief system that the apostles began to spread around 35 C.E. The 1st Century Christians were often forced to meet in secrecy because their teachings greatly clashed with orthodox Jewish beliefs. The Jewish authorities sought to stop the spread of Christianity by force. They authorized a Hellenized Jew, named Saul, to persecute and imprison Christians. However, Saul later became the most influential Christian figure of the 1st Century church, known as "the Apostle Paul."

Paul claimed that he personally met Jesus during a miraculous encounter on the road to Damascus and was commissioned by Jesus to be "a chosen vessel" to bear the name of Jesus "before the Gentiles, and kings, and the children of Israel." (Acts 9:15) Based on this encounter, Paul is counted as an apostle, the same as the original 12 apostles. Paul's first meeting with an original apostle was held three years after his conversion when he spent 15 days in Jerusalem with Peter. The teachings of Paul produced a conflict with

Jerusalem church leaders and he was pressured to leave Jerusalem.

Though the original apostles were personally trained and commissioned by Jesus to spread his teachings, Paul is credited with having done more to spread the religion then them. The New Testament of the Bible is composed of 27 books by seven writers, and 13 of them are believed to have been written by Paul.

The Bible confirms that Paul had the physical appearance of an Egyptian. In Acts 21:38 a Roman officer mistook Paul to be a certain Egyptian. Paul had to specify that he was a Jew. It appears that the Egyptians and Jews had physical characteristics indistinguishable to some Romans.

Paul's ministry emphasized the converting of Gentiles. In teaching these Christian proselytes, Paul was of the opinion that they did not have to observe all of the Jewish laws. Paul taught that Gentiles did not have to be circumcised and that they may eat food offered to idol gods. He de-emphasized observance of the Jewish laws.

Peter was the main leader of the apostles and James (also called James the Just), the brother of Jesus, became the head of the Christian community in Jerusalem. They represented a segment of 1st Century Christians called "Judaizers." Their belief in Jesus as the Messiah did not preclude their obedience of the Jewish laws. Non-Jewish converts to Christianity were expected to observe the Jewish laws, just as earlier proselytes.[83] This matter was the earliest major controversy to affect the new religion. During Paul's last visit to Jerusalem in 58 C.E., the Judaizers tried to kill him for teaching against the Jewish laws. Peter later accepted similar belief to Paul's.

The remainder of this chapter provides brief biographies of the most notable apostles, New Testament authors, deacons, disciples and believers who spread the Christian religion during the 1st Century. As Jews, they are all presumed to be Black people.

## *Apostles*

**Andrew**: He was a native of the fishing town Bethsaida, the brother of Simon Peter, and a former disciple of John the Baptist. He was one of the first

---

[83]Helmut Koester. *History and Literature of Early Christianity*. New York: Walter DeGruyter, 1987, p. 118.

disciples of Jesus. According to Eusebius, Andrew was sent to minister in Scythia.[84] *The Acts of St. Andrew*, an apocryphal writing, reports on his ministry and crucifixion in 60 C.E. at Patrae, a harbor city in Achaia.

**Bartholomew**: It is believed that he was also called Nathaniel in the Bible. According to tradition, he was killed in Armenia by persecutors who ripped the skin from his body.

**James, son of Alphaeus**: He was present in the Upper Room on the day of Pentecost. It is possible that he was the brother of Matthew. Nothing is known about his ministry after the crucifixion.

**James, son of Zebedee**: He was called "James the Great." He was the brother of John. James, Peter and John formed an inner circle of three men who were closest to Jesus. He was the first apostle to be put to death and the only apostle whose martyrdom is reported in the Bible (Acts 12). He was beheaded by Herod Agrippa.

**John**: He was the brother of James the Great and member of Jesus' inner circle, along with James and Peter. He and his brother were called "the sons of thunder" by Jesus. He reportedly led a ministry in Ephesus and was exiled to the Island of Patmos by Emperor Domitian. He is believed to be the author of the Gospel of John, 1 John, 2 John, 3 John and Revelations. Eusebius reports that he was put to death in Ephesus.

**Matthew**: He was a tax collector, recruited by Jesus from Capernaum. He is believed to be the author of the first gospel, based on the report of Papias, bishop of Hieropolis (60-130 C.E.), who stated that Matthew made a collection of the sayings of Jesus in Hebrew. One tradition reports of his martyrdom in Ethiopia.[85]

---

[84]Eusebius Pamphilus. *Ecclesiastical History*. Grand Rapid: Baker Book House, 1991, p. 82.

[85]Joan Comay and Ronald Brownrigg. *Who's Who in the Bible*. New York: Bonanza Books, 1980, p. 152. and Pamphilus, *Ecclesiastical History*, p. 127.

**Matthias**: He was a loyal disciple of Jesus before the crucifixion. He is mentioned only once in the Bible (Acts 1:12-26) as being chosen to replace Judas Iscariot, who hung himself after betraying Jesus. There is a tradition that places him in Ethiopia.

**Paul**: Formerly called Saul of Tarsus. He was a Hellenized Jew, and well trained in the Hebrew laws. He was a Roman citizen, a status not common to most Jews. He was the only apostle who did not know Jesus personally. He participated in the persecution of Christians and was responsible for the imprisonment and murder of many. He was converted to Christianity around 35 C.E. and ministered to the Gentile nations for about 30 years. He was the only apostle reported in the Bible to focus his ministry on the European nations. Because of his reputation as a persecutor of Christians, and because he did not require the Gentile converts to observe Jewish laws, he was hated among Christian and non-Christian Jews. Thirteen of the biblical Epistles identify him as the author, and some scholars believe him to be the author of the book of Hebrews. Sometime between 62 and 67 C.E., Paul was kept under house arrest in Rome, where he was allowed to receive guests and write many letters. Popular tradition says he was put to death in 67 C.E. by the Emperor Nero, who had him beheaded in or near Rome.

**Philip**: He was probably a disciple of John the Baptist and was recruited by Jesus by the River Jordan. One tradition says he died naturally at Hierapolis, while another tradition says he was crucified.

**Simon Peter**: He was a fisherman, as were John and James, and these three formed the inner circle closest to Jesus. Jesus called Peter a "rock" and said, "upon this rock I will build my church." Jesus personally commissioned him to "feed" his "sheep." Peter assumed the leadership of the apostles. The Bible reports that he did many miracles. His ministry was mainly to the Jews, just as Paul's was to the Gentiles. He was a Judaizer until he received a vision and determined that "...God shows no partiality, but in every nation anyone who fears him and does what is right is acceptable to him." (Acts 10:34-35) However, pressure from Judaizers forced him to temporarily discontinue ministering to Gentiles. He wrote a letter (1st Epistle of Peter) while in Babylon. This "Babylon" may refer figuratively to Rome. It may also refer literally to Babylon in the Mesopotamia, or the Babylon located in Egypt. There is great possibility that he was in Babylon, Egypt, because he mentions that Mark was with him. Mark is the traditional bishop to Egypt and founder of the Coptic (Egyptian) Church. This Babylon was also called "Old Cairo," and served as the main communication network between Near East Asia and Lower (Northern) Egypt.[86] It is widely believed that Peter also traveled to Rome, where he is traditionally considered the first Bishop of Rome. It was in Rome that he was crucified around 64 C.E.

**Simon, the Zealot**: He and Judas Iscariot are the only disciples believed to be members of the Zealots, a revolutionary faction of Jews. According to *The Passion of Simon and Jude*, an apocryphal writing, Simon's ministry and martyrdom took place in Persia.

**Thaddaeus**: Also called Judas, son of James. Nothing is known of his post-resurrection activities.

**Thomas**: Popularly known as "doubting Thomas" because of the doubts he had about the resurrection of Jesus. Tradition says he was a minister to Persia and southern India.

### *New Testament Authors*

**Matthew**: See page 76. He wrote the book of Matthew sometime between 68 and 72 C.E.

**Mark**: Also called John Mark. The church in Jerusalem met in his mother's home. He was a close friend to Simon Peter. The Gospel of Mark is believed to have been written by him, as told to him by Peter. He traveled with Paul and Barnabas on their first missionary journey in 45 C.E. During this journey, he left them in Perga and returned to Jerusalem, which greatly displeased Paul. It is believed that Mark was sent on his own missionary journey to take Christianity to Egypt where he is considered the founder of Egyptian Christianity and the first Bishop of Alexandria.[87] One tradition says

---

[86]Jill Kamil. *Coptic Egypt History and Guide*. Cairo: The American University in Cairo Press, 1987, p. 27.

[87]John S. Mbiti. *Introduction to African Religion*. London: Heinemann Educational Books, 1975, p. 182. and Han Conzelman. *History of Primitive Christianity*. New York: Abingdon Press, 1973, p. 115.

Mark was killed in Alexandria.[88] It is believed that he wrote the Gospel of Mark between 40 and 68 C.E.

**Luke**: He was from Antioch and is identified as a physician. His authorship of the Gospel of Luke and the Acts of the Apostles is widely accepted. These books were written to a Gentile official named Theophilus. It is assumed that Luke was Greek because of his name and the type of Greek he used when translating Aramaic words. However, Paul refers to Luke twice in his writings and never identifies him as a Greek, as he probably would have. Furthermore, Luke does not refer to himself as a Greek, which would have made his writings to Theophilus more personal, as one Gentile writing to another. He wrote the book of Luke and the Acts of the Apostles between 60 and 63 C.E.

**John**: See page 76. It is believed that he wrote the Gospel of John around 80 C.E.; 1 John, 2 John and 3 John around 90 C.E.; and Revelations around 96 C.E.

**Paul**: See page 77. It is believed that he wrote all of the letters (or epistles) credited to him between 52 C.E. to 67 C.E. The letters are Romans, 1 Corinthians, 2 Corinthians, Galatians, Ephesians, Philippians, Colossians, 1 Thessalonians, 2 Thessalonians, 1 Timothy, 2 Timothy, Titus, and Philemon. Some believe he also authored Hebrews.

**James, the Lord's Brother**: Also called "James the Just" and acknowledged by Paul as a "pillar of the Church." He was a son of Mary and Joseph and the brother of Jesus. He did not accept the teachings of Jesus until after the resurrection. He quickly became a leader in the Christian movement as the head of the church in Jerusalem, the capital city of Christianity and Judaism. He was a devout Judaizer, but he also had the respect of Christians who believed converted Gentiles did not have to follow the Jewish laws. Pressure from the high priest and Sanhedrin led to the execution of James in 62 C.E. He was thrown from the Temple wall into a ravine, and then clubbed to death. The letters ascribed to him were written to the 12 tribes of Israel. It is

---

[88]Birger A. Pearson and James E. Goehring, editors. *The Roots of Egyptian Christianity*. Philadelphia: Fortress Press, 1986, p. 141.

believed that he wrote the Epistle of James around 45 C.E.

**Peter**: See page 77. It is believed that he wrote 1 Peter around 63 C.E. and 2 Peter around 66 C.E.

**Jude**: Also called Judas. He was the brother of Jesus and James. He is not to be confused with Judas Iscariot or the apostle Judas. It is believed that he wrote the Epistle of Jude around 80 C.E.

***Disciples, Deacons, and Believers***

**Apollos**: By far, one of the most articulate and impressive leaders of the 1st Century. He was an Egyptian Jew from Alexandria. He and others that traveled with him were disciples of John the Baptist. He arrived in Ephesus in 53 C.E. (Acts 18:24) and taught in the synagogue. His teachings represented an excellent understanding of the Old Testament and the life of Jesus. He then traveled to Corinth where he attracted many people with his eloquent preaching. Some Corinthian Christians considered Apollos a rival of Paul, and factions developed between students of Apollos, Paul and Peter (Acts 19:1 and 1Corinthians1:12). Apollos later became the first Bishop of Corinth.

**Lucius of Cyrene**: He was from Libya, and an important leader of the church in Antioch.

**Philip the Evangelist**: One of seven deacons chosen to distribute charity to the poor of Jerusalem. His ministry produced many miracles. Philip met the chief treasurer for the Queen of Ethiopia, who was reading the Old Testament scriptures in his chariot. Philip related to him the teachings of Jesus.

**Simeon Niger**: The name "Niger" means Black and is likely an indication of the region of Africa he came from. He was an important official in the Christian church in Antioch.

**Simon of Cyrene**: An African from Libya who carried the cross of Jesus to Golgotha. His sons, Alexander and Rufus, were well known among 1st Century Christians.

**Stephen**: He was a Hellenized Jew and one of the seven deacons of Jerusalem. Stephen had a heated dispute with other Hellenized Jews that were members of the "Synagogue of the Freedmen" (or Libertines). Jews from Egypt and Asia Minor participated in this argument, as well. This argument led to Stephen being charged with blasphemy, and later stoned to death.

*Chapter 8*

# CHRISTIANITY INSTITUTIONALIZED IN AFRICA

The importance of Egypt to the life of Jesus is introduced early in the New Testament. According to Matthew 2:13-21, Joseph and Mary were divinely guided to take the newly born Jesus to Egypt to escape the wrath of Herod. A traditional site of Jesus' family is found in Old Cairo (called Babylon in the 1st Century), where the church of St. Sergius is located.[89] It is possible that Peter visited this Babylon and wrote his first letter while there.

The specific circumstances regarding the arrival of Christianity in Africa are not known. It is possible that the African Jews present at the day of Pentecost helped to spread the religion to their native lands.

The largest community of Jews outside of Palestine lived in Alexandria, Egypt. In fact, there were an estimated 200,000 Jews living in Alexandria and more than one million living throughout Lower (Northern) Egypt.[90] The apostles began their mission by reaching Jewish communities through the synagogues of the Roman Empire. Because of the large Jewish communities in Egypt, and easy access between Palestine and Egypt, it is only natural that the Jews of Alexandria were among the first to be introduced to Christianity.[91] Adolf von Harnack, historian of Christianity, is quoted as saying, "It is more than a conjecture that a larger number of Jews were converted to Christianity in the Nile Valley than anywhere else."[92]

---

[89]Otto F.A. Meinardus. *Christian Egypt Ancient and Modern.* Cairo: The American University in Cairo Press, 1977, p. 1.

[90]C.P. Groves. *The Planting of Christianity in Africa*. London: Lutterworth Press, 1948, p. 39.

[91]Helmut Koester. *History and Literature of Early Christianity*. New York: Walter De Gruyter, 1987, p. 220.

[92]Groves, *The Planting of Christianity in Africa*, p. 36.

According to popular tradition Mark (John Mark, author of the second Gospel) was sent as a missionary to Egypt by the apostles, possibly around 41 C.E. Mark's visits to Alexandria are reported by Clement of Alexandria and Eusebius.[93] An extra-biblical writing called the *Acts of Mark* provides a more detailed account of Mark's activities. It reports that Mark first traveled to Cyrene (Libya), where he performed many miracles. He then went to Alexandria. The first person he met was a shoemaker named Annianus (or Ananias). While repairing Mark's sandal he injured his left hand and cried out, "God is One." Mark healed Annianus' hand and related to him the gospel of Jesus.[94] This account may be fictitious or hyperbole, however, Eusebius lists Annianus as the first bishop of Alexandria.

It is interesting and somewhat macabre to note that the head of Mark remains in the Cathedral of St. Mark in Alexandria. Other skeletal parts, called "relics," are kept in Latin churches in Venice, Italy, France, Belgium and Germany.[95]

The ministry of Apollos (reported in Acts 18:24), an Alexandrian Jew, during the apostolic period provides biblical proof that Christianity had begun to spread in Alexandria during the first Century. Birger A. Pearson, author of an article titled "Earliest Christianity in Egypt: Some Observations," printed in *The Roots of Egyptian Christianity*, states the following:

> *It may nevertheless be interesting to note that the earliest documentable church, that of St. Theonas (bishop 282-300), lay in the northwestern part of the city, in the area we have identified as Delta, one of the "Jewish" quarters in the first century. This may imply a Jewish Christian presence in that area of the city before the time of the building of that church, and that presence could have extended back to the first century. As has already been indicated, the earliest Christians would have lived side by side with*

---

[93]Birger Pearson A. and James E. Goehring, editors. *The Roots of Egyptian Christianity*, Philadelphia: Fortress Press, 1986, pp. 138-139 and C. Wilfred Griggs. *Early Egyptian Christianity from Its Origins to 451 C.E.* New York: E.J. Brill, 1990, pp. 19-21.

[94]Ibid., p. 140.

[95]Meinardus, *Christian Egypt Ancient and Modern*, p. 28.

> *other Jews, sharing the life of the synagogues and worshiping in house churches.*[96]

Several factors contributed to the acceptance and growth of Christianity in Egypt during the 1st Century. Despite almost 1000 years of foreign rule in Egypt, Egyptian culture and beliefs remained very strong. Instead of ending the Pharaonic rule of Egypt, foreign leaders assumed rulership as Pharaohs. They had great respect for Egyptian civilization and sought to emulate its greatness. One of the most important surviving aspects of Egyptian civilization was its mythology.

The most important characters in Egyptian mythology are *Osiris*, *Isis* and *Horus* (or *Ausar*, *Auset* and *Huru*). This trio of Egyptian mythology is of similar status to God, Mary and Jesus in Christian theology. A more detailed examination of this issue is provided in Chapter 9. Cosmogonical, theological and mythological beliefs already established in Egypt made this region fertile for the planting of Christianity.

Philo, a 1st Century philosopher and Alexandrian Jew, reports the existence of a community of Egyptians called the *Therapeutae*. Philo was born in Alexandria around 15 B.C.E. He was a contemporary of Jesus and was reported to have conversed with Peter in Rome sometime between 41 C.E. and 54 C.E. According to Eusebius, the name *Therapeutae* may refer to the curing or healing of "the souls of those that came to them, thus ridding them, like a physician, of disorders bred of evil." Philo reports that the *Therapeutoe* (men of their community) and *Therapeutrides* (women of their community) were "exceedingly numerous in Egypt, in each of the nomes... and especially in the neighborhood of Alexandria." They renounced their property and moved to more solitary regions of the land. Each house in their communities had a sacred chamber, called the "holy place" or "monastery." In this room, an individual would bring no food, drink or anything for the body. The only items brought into the room were "laws, and inspired oracles from the lips of the prophets, and hymns and all else by which knowledge and piety are increased and perfected."[97] After dawn, they studied and meditated on sacred writings, "allegorizing the law of their fathers." Eusebius

---

[96]Pearson, *The Root of Egyptian Christianity*, pp. 151-152.

[97]Eusebius Pamphilus. *Ecclesiastical History*, Grand Rapids: Baker Book House, 1991, pp. 49-50.

adamantly espoused the opinion that these Egyptian sects were early Christians. Probably before the title "Christians" was popularly used.

1st Century Christianity represents the infancy of a growing religion that was born in the small Galilee region of the vast Roman Empire. Early Christians were a mere nuisance to the Empire. They upset the Jewish leaders, refused to worship the emperor, refused to worship other gods, and sold their property, which deprived the Roman Empire from its right to tax them. They began as a Jewish sect with allegiance to Jerusalem. They soon became an independent religious sect, persecuted by Jewish leaders and the Roman government.

The new religion produced holy men, holy scriptures and holy prophesies. There were also heretics, forged scriptures and false religions associated with Christianity. The religion spread throughout the Empire and experienced its greatest success in Egypt. It was there that the religion was nurtured and grew strong. Abraham went to Egypt a poor man and came out a wealthy man. Joseph entered Egypt a slave and became a great ruler. Jesus was taken into Egypt as a small child and came out the "Son of God," fulfilling the words of the prophet Hosea, "Out of Egypt have I called my son." (Hosea 11:1 and Matthew 2:15)

Christianity started in Galilee, but it was established and made strong in Egypt. The Egyptian contributions to Christianity are many. The greatest of the Church fathers were Africans; the first educational institution of the religion was in Egypt, started by an African; the monastic tradition began in Egypt, started by African men; the scriptures were translated and preserved for thousands of years in Egypt; and many of the ecumenical councils held to shape the future of the religion were influenced and controlled by Africans. For the first 400 years or more of Christianity, Africans played a pivotal role. The presence of Black people in the Bible, and the shaping of Christianity, is not the exception, it is the rule. True biblical history cannot exist void of African presence.

*Chapter 9*

# CHRISTIAN AND KEMETIC BELIEFS COMPARED

For many years, many Christian historians, theologians, and ministers have avoided connecting Christianity with Egyptian beliefs. Many Christians believe that all Egyptian beliefs are false, evil, satanic, idolatrous and/or ungodly. Many people respond to what they don't understand with fear and hatred. The connections between Christianity and Egyptian beliefs are blatantly obvious. To ignore these connections is like acknowledging a tree and joyfully eating its fruit, while simultaneously ignoring or hating its roots.

Early Christian theologians have been accused of "stealing" their theology from the Egyptians, the same as the Greeks "stole" philosophy from Egypt. Based on this charge, some people reject Christianity as a false religion. This accusation is becoming more popular and causing many to look upon the religion suspiciously.

This chapter provides an examination of connections between Christian theology and certain Egyptian cosmogonies, mythologies and theologies. This text does not provide an exhaustive analysis of Egyptian belief, which would require many volumes of books. Instead, certain Christian theological beliefs are compared to ancient Egyptian beliefs.

For many years it was popularly believed that God created Adam and Eve about 5,000 years ago. This belief in a 5,000-year-old humanity has been rejected by modern theologians and scientists, placed in the same category as believing that the sun revolved around a flat earth. To acknowledge that humanity was created more than 5,000 years ago is the first step toward understanding the continuity of beliefs from Egyptian to Christian.

Scientists estimate human lineage began more than 2.5 million years ago in Africa with a species called *Homo habilis*. They believe that the first modern humans existed between 100,000 to 200,000 years ago.[98] Biblical history begins about 5,000 years ago with no references to humanity existing before Adam. It must be concluded that belief in a 5,000-year-old humanity

---

[98]*Newsweek*, "The Search for Adam and Eve" by John Tierney, January 11, 1988, pp. 46-52 and *U.S. News and World Report*, "Who We Were" by William F. Allman, September 16, 1991, pp. 53-60.

is in error. The dismissal of this belief produces a question; that is, "How was the Creator viewed by humans more than 5,000 years ago?"

It is not possible to know all of the religions that have existed since the creating of humanity. However, the beliefs held by the ancient Egyptians are made known to us through the histories recorded in the pyramids, papyrus records and popular myths. These beliefs pre-date Christianity by more than 5,000 years and remained popular in Egypt into the 4th Century. According to Saint Augustine, "It must be confessed that before Moses there had already been, not indeed among the Greeks, but among the barbarous nations, as in Egypt, some doctrine which might be called their wisdom, else it would not have been written in the holy books that Moses was learned in all the wisdom of the Egyptians."[99] The biblical creation account, presumably written by Moses, begins with God creating the earth, making it "without form and void," somehow composed of "waters." God then created light, separated the waters with a firmament (or atmosphere), formed the earth land masses, created various life forms and then created man. This is somewhat similar to ancient Egyptian cosmogony, which taught the eternal existence of primordial matter that was not created. This matter was called *Nun*. Somehow, *Nun* became self-aware and began to bring the mass of primordial matter into order, creating the world. At this point the *Nun* becomes *Ra*, the first God.[100] The first creations of *Ra* were four divine pairs. These pairs were *Shu* and *Tefnut* or air and humidity; *Geb* and *Nut* or earth and heaven; *Osiris* and *Isis*, the fertile human couple to beget humanity; and *Seth* and *Nephthys*, the infertile couple that would bring evil to humanity. According to John 1:1, it was through the Word that was "with God" and "was God," that all things were made. Similarly, it was through the *Ka* (universal reason) that *Ra* created the world. The use of *Ka* in Egyptian cosmogony is equivalent to the use of the *logos* (Greek for Word) in this scripture. So far, the God of Egyptian cosmogony is represented in three different forms. These forms are the *Nun*, *Ra* and *Ka*. The Egyptians interpreted these and other representations as distinct and different aspects of the one Supreme

---

[99]Saint Augustine. *The City of God*. New York: The Modern Library of Random House, 1950, p. 646.

[100]Cheikh Anta Diop. *Civilization or Barbarism*. Brooklyn: Lawrence Hill Books, 1991, pp. 310-311.

God. In Genesis, God is quoted as saying "Let us make man...." This use of "us" obviously implies plurality. It could be compared to the many aspects of God, referred to by the Egyptians as the *Netcherw* collectively or *Netcher* individually. The word nature is derived from this word. It has been translated to mean "god-like," "holy," "divine," "sacred," "power," "strength," "force," "strong," "fortify," "mighty," and "protect."[101] In Genesis, the making of man out of dust, and the words of Isaiah 64:8, "...we are the clay, and you are our potter," are often compared to the making of man by the *Netcher Khunum*. Thousands of years before the writing of Genesis, Khunum was portrayed sitting at a potter's table forming the *Ba* and *Ka* of humanity. The murder of Abel by Cain in Genesis can be compared to the murder of Osiris, by his jealous brother Seth.

The Egyptians believed that there were certain truths that could not be explained through simple sciences and history. These truths represent Egyptian sciences, histories, religions, mathematics, philosophies and spirituality. The myths were developed to represent these truths and to express complicated belief systems. Many cultures use allegories and metaphors to express certain ideas. The use of myths was the highest form of this expression of ideas.

Over thousands of years, popular *Osirian* myths developed in Egypt. The myths are variations of the same general story. According to the myth, *Osiris* was the fertile man created by *Ra*. His infertile brother, *Seth*, became jealous of him and plotted to kill him. Through trickery, *Seth* trapped Osiris inside a chest and threw him into the Nile River. The chest was later found by *Isis*, the wife of *Osiris*. When *Seth* realized that the body of *Osiris* was found, he was able to recapture it, cut it into 14 pieces, and scatter them across the land. *Isis* was able to recover 13 of the pieces.

*Isis* was given certain words by the *Netcher Thoth*. *Thoth* represents divine articulation of speech and truth. When *Isis* spoke these words to the dismembered body of *Osiris*, she received the seed (sperm) of *Osiris* and became pregnant, giving birth to *Horus*. This conception is the oldest story of a virgin birth in history. For this reason, *Horus* was mocked and considered deformed because he was born of the seed of someone who was dead. The

---

[101]E.A. Wallis Budge. *The Book of the Dead*. Secaucus, NJ: Universal Books, Inc. 1960) pp. 99-100 and Anthony T. Browder. *Nile Valley Contributions to Civilization*. Washington D.C.: The Institute of Karmic Guidance, 1992, p. 83.

incantations spoken by *Isis* led to the resurrection of *Osiris*, who ultimately became the judge of the departed souls, seated on the Throne of Judgement. The same as Jesus serving as "judge" of "the living and dead," as stated in the Apostle's Creed. When *Horus* matured, he had many battles with *Seth* to avenge the murder of his father. *Horus* became the victor over *Seth* and represents the triumph of good over evil.[102]

It was this ancient Osirian myth that was taught to Moses (Acts 7:22), and later told to Alexander the Great more than 300 years before the Christian era.[103] As a people from Egypt, the Israelites were well acquainted with the worship of Isis and the Osirian myths. According to Jill Kamil, author of *Coptic Egypt History and Guide*, "The cult of Egypt's most beloved goddess Isis exerted a strong influence on the early church, and particularly on Coptic Christianity."[104]

When comparing the life of Jesus with that of Horus, we learn that both were born of a virgin, baptized at the age of 30, share December 25th as a birth date, and each are referred to as "the Son of God." Portrayals of an infant Horus in the arms of his mother are the earliest forms of a Madonna and child, and pre-date Jesus by more than 3,000 years. Osiris and Jesus are similar in that both were violently killed and then resurrected, and both are characterized as God judging the souls of humanity.

In Revelations 3:14 Jesus is called the "Amen, the faithful and true witness, the beginning of the creation of God." In Egyptian cosmogonies, *Amen* is the *Netcher* used by *Ra* to create the other *Netcherw*. There are also commonalities between *Seth* (also *Set* or *Seti*) and Satan. They both represent all that is evil and against the nature of God.

Long before the Christian era, the Egyptians believed in one true and supreme God, the creation of humanity, resurrection of the body, life after physical death, the judging of the soul, the virgin birth and the victory of good over evil. They also lived according to certain laws called the *Declarations of Innocence* or *Admonitions of Maat*. The Declarations were

---

[102]Ibid., p. 89 and Jill Kamil. *Coptic Egypt History and Guide*. Cairo: The American University in Cairo Press, 1987, p. 30.

[103]Augustine, *The City of God*, p. 279.

[104]Kamil, *Coptic Egypt History and Guide*, p. 29.

composed of more than 147 "negative confessions," which were learned by the Egyptians in preparation for their day of judgement before *Osiris*. On that day, the deceased would declare "I have not stolen," "I have done no murder," "I have not spoken lies," "I have not committed fornication," "I have not defiled the wife of any other man," and so on. These negative confessions pre-date the Ten Commandments by thousands of years.[105]

Another important indication of Egyptian influence on early Christianity is the use of the ankh as a symbol of the cross by Coptic Christians. The ankh is an Osirian symbol of eternal life from the Early Dynastic Period. In early Christianity it retained its meaning as a symbol of Eternal life. According to Jack Tresidder, the author of *The Complete Dictionary of Symbols*, (Chronical Books, 2005), "Its shape has been variously understood as the rising sun on the horizon, as the union of male and female, or other opposites, and also as a key to esoteric knowledge and to the afterworld of the spirit." The Coptic Church utilized the ankh as a form of the Christian cross, symbolizing eternal life through Christ. In the 4th Century, the Church began to use the symbol without the circular upper part, replacing it with a straight top.

Even if early Christians in Palestine were completely unaware of Egyptian beliefs, the Jews and Christians of Egypt were completely aware of the myths. It is obvious that Egyptian beliefs influenced the development of the Christian religion. The similarities may have developed naturally because the Israelites were originally from Egypt. Early Christians may have taken from Egyptian beliefs and claimed them as their own. The similarities may be expressions of the same God and beliefs as experienced by two different cultures. In any case, the beliefs represent a truth far greater than any religion.

---

[105] Amon Saba Saakana, editor. *The Afrikan Origin of the Major World Religions*. London: Karnak House 1988, pp. 25-26.

*Chapter 10*

# FATHERS OF THE CHRISTIAN CHURCH

During the 1st Century, the apostles and their disciples facilitated the spread of Christianity. As these apostolic fathers passed on, Christianity continued to grow and change. A Zealot-led rebellion against the Romans resulted in the total destruction of Jerusalem in 70 C.E. and Antioch became the primary center for Christianity in Palestine. Christians suffered periods of persecution under different Emperors for almost 400 years and church meetings were often held in secret. The growth of Christianity did not happen with the support of the Roman government. It grew in spite of often brutal Roman opposition. Despite the New Testament emphasis on European and Palestinian Christian communities, it was in North Africa that Christianity truly matured. The Roman church made very few, if any, significant contribution to early Christianity.

The development of the Christian church after the 1st Century was largely guided by certain men. The contributions of these men to Christian theology, history and practices are invaluable. They have earned the recognition of the Christian world as the Fathers of the Christian Church and most of them were Africans.

The eight men presented in this chapter were not the only ones to influence the development of Christianity, but they are among the most notable church fathers. Their names are Basilides, Valentinus, Pantaenus, Tertullian, Origen, Cyprian, Athanasius, and Augustine. These men are held in high esteem in Christian history. However, their heritage as Africans is usually omitted from the historical record. Like most biblical figures, they are often falsely portrayed as white. Since Africans are generally identified as Black people, we are safe to identify these eight men as Black.

Historical documentation verifying their race differs from one person to the next. Criteria used to conclude that they were Black men include: 1) being born in Africa; 2) born of African parents (who are usually referred to as "pagan parents" in many Church history texts); 3) they wrote and spoke non-European languages; 4) acknowledged their African heritage in their own writings; 5) called "African" by other writers; or 6) had names that reflect African beliefs.

### *Basilides*

He was an Alexandrian Christian teacher during the earlier part of the 2nd Century (around 125 C.E.) and claimed an apostolic succession through the apostle Matthias.[106] He was the first to write a commentary on the gospels and the founder of the first school of gnostic Christianity in Alexandria. Gnostics taught that those initiated into its mysteries gained salvation through special knowledge (*gnosis* in Greek) revealed by a spiritual savior.

Basilides taught that divine life unfolds in seven successive stages and that man has two souls, one rational trying to dominate the other one, which is animal or material. He also believed that a "nonexistent God" produced a "nonexistent seed," and from this seed "existent things" were produced. One of the existent things produced was a "threefold Sonship" whose goal was to return to the nonexistent God.[107] Salvation would be achieved when the Sonship is brought into eternal rest in its proper position. These beliefs were classified as heretical. However, they were accepted by many early Christians and the presence of followers of Basilides continued into the 4th Century C.E.

### *Valentinus*

He was a gnostic teacher and poet born in Egypt and probably educated in Alexandria. He taught in Egypt before traveling to Rome around 140 C.E. Only fragments of his writings remain. However, it is possible that he is the author of the *Gospel of Truth*, one of the books found near Nag Hammadi in Upper Egypt. The gnostic schools founded by him are considered more impressive than that of his predecessor, Basilides.

Valentinus taught that Jesus shared knowledge with the disciples not shared with the masses. Jesus said, "Unto you it is given to know the mysteries of the kingdom of God: but to others in parables; that seeing they may not see, and hearing they may not understand."[108] These mysteries were

---

[106]Robert M. Grant. *Second-Century Christianity*. London: The Trustees of the Society for Promoting Christian Knowledge, 1957, p. 19.

[107]Robert M. Grant. *Augustus to Constantine*. New York: Harper & Row, Publishers, 1970, p. 125 and Helmut Koester. *History and Literature of Early Christianity*. New York: Walter De Gruyter, 1987, p. 232.

[108]Elaine Pagels. *The Gnostic Gospels*. New York: Random House, 1979, p. 14

taught to certain believers by the apostles and their students. Valentinus claimed that he learned the mysteries from Theudas, a student of Paul. He also taught that there were three classes of human beings. The highest form of human was *pneumatikoi*, a spiritual person; the second was *psychikoi*, one that merely possesses a soul; and the lowest form was hylikoi, one that was only matter and void of spirit or soul.[109] The most notable student of Valentinus was Origen, and Valentinians were present into the 4th Century.

***Pantaenus*** (120 to 200 C.E.)

He was the founder and first head of the *Didascalia*, the world-famous Catechetical School in Alexandria. It was the first educational center established to instruct its students in proper orthodox Christian theology. As the most known and highly respected institution of Christian thought, it had no rival. Eusebius describes Pantaenus as "one of the most eminent teachers of his day" and a stoic philosopher. His teaching was so eloquent that he was sent to India to preach the gospel to the people of the East.[110] The brilliance of his lectures attracted many students, including Clements of Alexandria, another great church father.

***Tertullian*** (155 to 245 C.E.)

His full name was Quintus Septimius Florens Tertullian. He was born in Carthage and trained as a lawyer. Around 198 C.E., while practicing law in Rome, he became a Christian and moved back to Carthage. Shortly after returning home, he was made a presbyter. Eusebius called him "one of the most brilliant men in Rome."[111]

Tertullian was the first to popularize the use of Latin in writing Christian literature and Harnack stated that "Tertullian in fact created Christian Latin literature....Cyprian polished the language...Augustine, again, stood on the

---

and *The Original African Heritage Study Bible*, King James Version. Nashville: James C. Winston Publishing Company, 1993, Luke 8:10.

[109]Koester, *History and Literature of Early Christianity*, p. 233.

[110]G.A. Williamson, translator. *Eusebius: The History of the Church from Christ to Constantine*. Minneapolis: Augsburg Publishing House, 1965, p. 213.

[111]Ibid., p. 75.

shoulders of Tertullian and Cyprian these three North Africans are the fathers of the Western Churches."[112] His many writings were systematic, precise and polemical. Around 203 C.E. he became a Montanist. The Montanists expected the return of Jesus during their time. They lived strict and disciplined lives of prayer, fasting, celibacy and regarded martyrdom as a most honorable service. Tertullian was the most notable Montanist convert.

The decision of Callistus, the Bishop of Rome, to absolve and remit the sins of penitent adulterers and fornicators caused a great deal of controversy. Tertullian taught that there were seven unforgivable sins that would exclude Christians from the Church without the possibility of re-admission. These sins were murder, idolatry, theft, apostasy, blasphemy, fornication and adultery. He believed that Callistus' decision lowered church standards.[113] The decision of Callistus was ultimately accepted by the Church over the objections of Tertullian.

Other theological issues expounded on and popularized by Tertullian include the trinity of the Father (God), Son (Jesus) and the Holy Spirit; baptism; the Lord's Prayer; forms of worship; and repentance. He explained his Christian beliefs with this paradox: "The Son of God was born, I am not ashamed of it because it is shameful; the Son of God died, it is credible for the very reason that it is silly; and, having been buried, he rose again, it is certain because it is impossible."[114]

***Origen*** (186 to 255 C.E.)

Also called Origines Adametius, he was born in Alexandria and became a very serious and famous Christian writer and teacher. The name "Origen" is derived from the Egyptian god Horus and may indicate that he was born on the anniversary of Horus.[115]

---

[112]David Ayerst and A.S.T. Fisher. *Records of Christianity, Volume I.* Oxford: Basil Blackwell, pp. 94-95.

[113]Edwyn Beven. *Christianity*. London: Oxford University Press, 1932, pp. 78-79.

[114]Ayerst, *Records of Christianity*, p. 95.

[115]John Ernest Leonard Oulton and Henry Chadwick, translators. *Alexandrian Christianity*. Philadelphia: The Westminster Press, p. 171.

As a child his family lived under the rule of the Emperor Septimius Severus, who was also an African. Origen was trained in the scriptures by his father, Leonides. A great love for the Christian faith was nurtured in him by his father's teachings. Severus made laws forbidding Christians and Jews from making new converts. Leonides was arrested and subsequently martyred for violating these laws.

Origen was close to 16 when his father was killed. Eusebius described him as having "an ambition extraordinary in one so young" and "an enthusiasm beyond his years."[116] The martyrdom of his father greatly affected him. He longed for the opportunity to give his life for the cause of Christ and often placed himself in situations that would have naturally led to him being stoned to death. However, he was always miraculously saved from death. His fearlessness encouraged thousands of Christians to boldly face martyrdom.

He became the most brilliant student of Clement at the Catechetical School in Alexandria and succeeded Clement as the head of the school. Origen subjected himself to extreme methods of discipline, which included long periods of fasting, sleep deprivation and poverty. His most extreme action was self-mutilation. Heeding the words of Matthew that, "There be eunuchs, which made themselves eunuchs for the kingdom of heaven's sake" (Matthew 19:12), Origen cut off his penis.

Because of his zeal and expertise in Christian theology, his fame spread throughout the Christian world. He was invited to Arabia and Palestine to lecture. About 215 C.E. he spoke at the church in Caesarea. It was rare for a layman to be invited to speak in a church, as this honor was usually given to ordained clerics. His speaking in the church displeased Demetrius, the Bishop of Alexandria. Origen was promptly ordered to return to Alexandria, where he continued to teach for 15 years. Around 232 C.E. he left Alexandria and was made a presbyter by the Bishops of Caesarea. His rise as an ordained minister was opposed by Demetrius, who held a meeting of bishops and they rejected the ordaining of Origen because of his act of self-mutilation.[117]

Neither the opposition of Demetrius or the persecution of Severus broke

---

[116]Williamson, *Eusebiu:s The History of the Church from Christ to Constantine*, pp. 240,244.

[117]Oulton, *Alexandrian Christianity*, pp. 175-176.

the spirit and will of Origen, who continued to serve the Church and grow in fame. He traveled for several years and then settled in Caesarea, where he established a second catechetical school. Many of the students trained by him became high church officials and theologians.

His writings include a commentary on the book of John, *De Principiis*, *Homilies*, *Of Origins*, *On Martyrdom*, and his *Hexapla*. The *Hexapla* presented the Old Testament in the original Hebrew with a Greek transliteration, a Greek version of the Septuagint, Aquila, Symmachus and Theodotion, all arranged in six parallel columns.

In 249 C.E. Origen was tortured under the persecution of the Emperor Decius. He survived this torture and lived for six more years before dying in 255 C.E. Harnack is quoted as saying that "all thinkers were under his influence" in the Christian world of the 4th Century.[118]

In later years, some of the teachings of Origen were declared heretical. Augustine challenged Origen's opinion of the nature of sin and reincarnation presented in *Of Origins*.[119] His doctrines became increasingly viewed as more controversial during the Middle Ages.

***Cyprian*** (200 to 258 C.E.)

Also called Thascius Caecilius Cyprianus. Little is known of his early years. The historical accounts regarding him begin around 240 C.E. At that time, he was a Carthaginian landowner and trained in Roman law. He had a reputation of being an excellent orator. When he became a Christian, he sold his material goods and gave the money to the poor, which was an act popular among the apostles and many early Christians. In 249 C.E. he was ordained a presbyter and shortly after replaced Donatus as the Bishop of Carthage.[120]

From 250 to 251 C.E. the persecution of Christians by Emperor Decius forced him into exile, and he continued to guide his church by correspondence. When he returned, he was confronted with a controversy

---

[118]Beven, *Christianity*, p. 77.

[119]Saint Augustine. *The City of God*. New York: The Modern Library of Random House, 1950, pp. 366-368.

[120]G.W.Clarke, translator. *The Letters of St. Cyprian of Carthage*. New York: Newman Press, 1950, pp. 14-15.

regarding the *lapsi*. The lapsi were those Christians who rejected their faith during the persecution and many of them wanted to be re-admitted into the Church. The issue produced two opposing parties. One group favored lax treatment of the lapsi and another that demanded severe treatment. Cyprian insisted on an act of penance from the lapsi, before the possibility of absolution would be allowed. This approach didn't satisfy either party and the matter was never completely settled.

The controversy continued and expanded when the presbyter Novatianus, the leader of those who wanted the lapsi to be treated severely, opposed the appointment of Cornelius as the Bishop of Rome. Cyprian supported the appointment. Cornelius served for three years and was succeeded by Lucius, who died after eight months as bishop.

In 254 C.E. Cyprian was at odds with Stephen, the successor of Lucius as the bishop of Rome. The issue was whether baptism administered to someone by one declared a heretic was valid. Stephen, along with other church leaders in Rome and Alexandria, considered the baptisms valid as long as water was used, and the candidate followed the proper rituals. According to Tertullian, these rituals included prayer, fasting and an all-night vigil the day before the rite; confession of all sins; a repudiation of Satan and his angels; an anointing with oil; the taking of milk and honey; three immersions into the water; and a confession of faith in God, Jesus and the Holy Spirit. Cyprian argued that a person baptized by a heretic must be baptized again, while Stephen upheld the tradition of prayer and a "laying on of hands" of these Christians.[121]

In 256 C.E. Cyprian became involved in another issue that would not be settled until long after his death and would greatly affect the future of the Christian world. It was the question of Roman judicial authority over other bishops. From the 1st to the 4th Century, three main centers of Christianity emerged. They were Alexandria in Egypt, Antioch in Syria, and Rome in Italy. The bishops of these cities were more powerful than those of smaller sees and began to exert power over them.

Cyprian challenged the power of the Bishop of Rome over other sees. He argued that episcopal authority originated with Jesus, who first passed it to

---

[121]Kenneth Scott Latourette. *A History of Christianity Vol.I.* New York: Harper & Row Publishers, 1975, pp. 194-196 and Williamson, *Eusebius: The History of the Church from Christ to Constantine*, p. 288.

Peter and then to the other apostles. This authority was then passed on by the apostles to their students, who continued to pass it on over the years. This same authority was shared equally by all bishops, according to Cyprian and was not the sole property of any particular bishop.[122] Therefore, the unity of the Church rested in this shared authority, and all people outside of the Church were not true Christians. In later years the supremacy of the See of Rome was forced on the Christian world by authority of the Roman government.

The persecution of Christians was renewed in 257 C.E. by Emperor Valerian. Cyprian bravely accepted martyrdom on September 14, 258 C.E. Before being beheaded he thanked those who sentenced him to death and gave 25 pieces of gold to his executioner.[123]

***Athanasius*** (293 to 373 C.E.)

He was born in Upper Egypt (southern Egypt) and raised by his parent for church service. He rose through the ranks of church leadership to become Bishop of Alexandria in 319 C.E. He chose to spend much of the first six years of his episcopate among the monastic circles, and Christian communities of the desert regents along the Nile River and Libyan border. It's interesting to note that church historian Justo Gonzalez refers to Athanasius as being called "the Black Dwarf."[124] Presumably, this nickname is based on the words of Julian the Apostate who wrote in his *Letter to the Alexandrians*, that Athanasius was a "common little fellow." The Greek term Julian uses is *anthropoikos* and is interpreted to mean little in stature. Though there is no statement about his skin color, his Blackness in assumed because of his Egyptian heritage.

His 47 years as bishop started with a controversy that began with his predecessor, Alexander. The matter was initiated by an Egyptian presbyter

---

[122]Beven, *Christianity*, p. 112 and Latourette, *A History of Christianity Vol.I*, p. 133.

[123]J.C. deGraft-Johnson. *African Glory*. Baltimore: Black Classic Press, 1954, p. 42.

[124]Justo L. Gonzalez. *The Story of Christianity, Volume 1*. Harper One, 2010, p.199.

named Arius. Arius challenged the opinion of Origen that the Son of God was of a "eternal, timeless generation." Arius argued that a generation cannot be "timeless" and that there must have been a point when the generation of Christ began. Athanasius held that if the Son was not eternal, he was subject to change. This nature of being subject to change makes Christ inconsistent and the possibility of eternal salvation unstable. This issue became known as the Arian controversy, and it led to the Council of Nicea in 325 C.E.

The Council of Nicea upheld the opinion of Athanasius, which resulted in the establishing of the *Nicene Creed.* Yet, the controversy was far from over. Arius used his political connections with the Roman government, which began a period of toleration of Christianity in 313 C.E., to hold another council meeting in Tyre in 335 C.E. The council was dominated by supporters of Arian and had the enforcement of Emperor Constantine. It resulted in Athanasius being deposed as bishop and banished to Gaul for three years. This was the first of five exiles that Athanasius suffered from 335 to 363 C.E., because of this controversy. Christian history recognizes him as the "Father of Orthodoxy." Athanasius was a prolific writer and provided the first listing of the 27 New Testament books (Matthew though Revelation) as they occur in the present canon of the Bible. He also issued an order purging all heretical writings.[125] He wrote *The Life of St. Antony* in 357 C.E., which spread throughout the Christian world and greatly inspired many people.

***Augustine*** (354 to 430 C.E.)

Also called Aurelius Augustinus. He is regarded as the greatest of the Fathers of the Church and served as the Bishop of Hippo in Africa. He was born in Tagaste, Numidia, and was educated in Madaura (not far from Tagaste) and Carthage. As a young man he studied astrology, Aristotle, Plato, neoplatonism and skepticism. He had great appreciation for the Latin language, which he accepted as a second language, but considered Greek difficult and too foreign.[126] While rejecting Christianity, he became a member of the Manicheans, a North African sect of Gnosticism that taught a form of radical dualism.

He first taught in Tagaste, where he started his family, and then in

---

[125]Pagels, *The Gnostic Gospels*, p. 120.

[126]degraft-Johnson, *African Glory*, p. 44.

Carthage before moving to teach in Rome at the age of 29 in 383 C.E. He soon learned of a position in Milan as Master of Rhetoric. Milan had replaced Rome as the new center for imperial government. Augustine succeeded in gaining this position over several other candidates. It was in Milan that he met St. Ambrose and ultimately became a Christian.

While struggling to overcome an overactive sex drive, Augustine sought solitude in a quiet garden, where he heard a child's voice say "take, read." There he found a copy of the Letter to the Romans, and read in the 13th chapter, verses 13 and 14, "not in rioting and drunkenness, not in chambering and wantonness, not in strife and envying, but put on the Lord Jesus Christ, and make not provision for the flesh, to fulfil the flesh thereof."[127] In addition to his conversion experience, his acceptance of Christianity was also influenced by his mother, a highly spiritual Christian woman. She visited him in Italy after his conversion and was proud of his accomplishments. His mother died while returning to Africa and his joy turned to pain.

Augustine returned to Africa, intending to start a monastery. However, he was immediately and aggressively entreated to accept the position of Bishop of Hippo in North Africa. He accepted this church office in 395 C.E. Though he was a Bishop and priest, he lived his life as a monk. He ordered his episcopal headquarters like a cenobitic monastery and committed himself to a life of spiritual pursuit like a monk.

Pelaguis, a British monk, initiated one of the first church controversies that Augustine participated in. Pelaguis taught that eternal life could be gained without the grace of God provided through Jesus if a person lived a "stainless" life. This teaching violated an orthodox belief in the "original sin," which was first stated in Romans 5:12. It was commonly believed that sin entered humanity through the disobedience of Adam and Eve. This original sin was passed on to all humanity and forgiven by the grace of God given through Jesus. Augustine led the fight against Pelaguis' heresy, which was condemned by the Council of Ephesus. Augustine's success in this matter earned him recognition as the "Doctor of Grace."[128]

He also gained respect in his challenge to the Arians and Manichaeans.

---

[127]Latourette, *A History of Christianity Vol.I*, pp. 96-97.

[128]Martin P. Harney. *The Catholic Church Through the Ages*. Boston: Daughters of St. Paul, 1974, pp. 61-62.

His voluminous writings included 93 major works, 263 sermons and 260 letters. His two most revered and celebrated writings are his *Confessions*, an autobiography of his struggles for conversion, and *The City of God*, a theological explanation for historical events. Through his writings, he defended Christianity against those who blamed the religion for the fall of the Roman Empire. In his *Expositions of the Psalms*, he eloquently encouraged Christians in their duty to each other with these words: "The man you cannot put right is still yours. He is part of you; either as a fellow human being, or very often as a member of your church, he is inside with you....Strive humbly to be what you would have him be, and you will not think that he is what you are not."[129]

In 410 C.E. Rome was invaded by the barbaric Goths, led by Alaric, an Arian Christian. The Arian movement started with the Egyptian presbyter Arius. Initially the Arians were those who theologically and politically sided with the position on the nature of Christ held by Arius, and against the position of Athanasius and those who subsequently supported his position. Over time, the term Arian lost some of its nontrinitarian theological purpose and became a nationalistic term, similar to how the Irish Catholics and Irish Protestants use these religious designations to identify their respective political positions.

However, whether or not the term "Arian," as used by the Germanic tribes (i.e., Goths and Vandals), has anything to do with the use of "Aryan" by the Nazis, is uncertain. It makes sense that they would use the term "Arian" as a way to emulate and celebrate the Germanic tribes that conquered the Roman Empire. It makes little sense that they would "go against the grain" of their "master race" philosophy and choose a term from a people of color to describe themselves. The Nazi's argue that it is from the Sanskrit term *arya* and means "honorable" or "noble." Either way, a Black heritage is probably involved whether it is from a Black Egyptian presbyter from the 4th Century C.E., or Black India from before 1000 B.C.E. But let's get back to the Goths.

The Goth's siege produced great hunger in Rome and some people resorted to cannibalism to survive. Jerome, a Palestinian monk, reports the desperation of the Romans in his letter titled *Jerome to Principia*, where he writes "The rage of hunger had recourse to impious food; men tore one

---

[129]Ayerst, *Records of Christianity*, p. 288.

another's limbs, and the mother did not spare the baby at her breast, taking again within her body that which her body had just brought forth."[130]

In 429 C.E. the Vandals invaded North Africa. Like the Goths, the Vandals were Gothic-speaking Arian Christians with white skin and blond hair. They focused much of their attention on destroying churches, basilicas, cemeteries, monasteries and houses of prayer. Augustine died in 430 from an illness while Hippo remained under siege until 439 C.E.

[130]Ibid., p. 295.

*Chapter 11*

# CHRISTIAN EDUCATION

In Alexandria, Egypt, the first institution of Christian education was established sometime around 180 C.E. by Pantaenus. It was called the Didascalia or Catechetical School. As these names imply, it provided a didactic method of presenting Christian theology to its catechumens (students being prepared for church membership). In addition to theology, the students studied philosophy and literature. They also copied scriptural manuscripts for distribution throughout the Christian world.[131] The school probably began with Pantaenus attracting a small group of young men with his teachings, but it grew to be the greatest institution for orthodox Christian education of its time.

When Pantaenus died around 200 C.E., Clement of Alexandria became the next head of the Didascalia. He was one of Pantaenus' best students, but little is known of his short tenure as head of the school. It is believed that he was born in Athens around 150 C.E. and came to Alexandria around 180 C.E. Clement left Egypt around 203 C.E. to escape a period of persecution started by Septimius Severus. He went on to become a great theologian and writer.

The next to head the school was Origen, a 17-year-old who studied under Pantaenus and Clement. Demetrius, the Bishop of Alexandria, appointed Origen as head of the school because of his reputation of being precocious, a very competent teacher and zealous in spite of the persecuting of Christians. The school grew in quality and quantity, teaching men and women under the leadership of Origen.[132] His fame spread throughout the Christian world, and he was often invited to teach abroad.

Around 231 C.E., Origen resigned his position as head of the Didascalia. The reason for his departure was most likely due to increasing conflicts with Demetrius. He continued to serve the Church while living in Caesarea in Palestine, and also started another catechetical school there.

---

[131] Otto F.A. Meinardus. *Christian Egypt Ancient and Modern.* Cairo: The American University in Cairo, 1977 p. 4.

[132] John Ernest Leonard Oulton and Henry Chadwick, translators. *Alexandrian Christianity.* Philadelphia: The Westminster Press, pp. 173-174.

Origen was succeeded by his best student, Heracles, who shortly thereafter replaced Demetrius when he died in 231 C.E. as Bishop of Alexandria. Heracles was responsible for teaching the lower level students, while Origen taught the more advanced students. Eusebius described Heracles as "a remarkable example of the philosophic (ascetic) life and discipline."[133]

Leadership of the Didascalia was then gained by another of Origen's best students, Dionysius of Alexandria. He continued as head of the school until 248 C.E. when he became Bishop of Alexandria. Little is known about the history of the school after Dionysius. It continued beyond the 4th Century and heads of the school included Theognostus, Prierus, Achillas and Peter of Alexandria.

Though the Didascalia was not like the large, modern Christian institutions of today, it produced the greatest Christian theologians in history.

---

[133]G.A. Williamson, translator. *Eusebius: The History of the Church from Christ to Constantine*. Minneapolis: Augsburg Publishing House, 1965) p. 242.

*Chapter 12*

# CHRISTIAN MONASTICISM

The word "monk" seldom evokes the image of an African man living a life of prayer, solitude and service. However, the monastic tradition has its deepest roots in the sands of the Egyptian deserts. The ascetic lifestyle had its origin in Egypt long before the founding of Christian monasticism.

The three basic kinds of monastic lifestyles are the eremite, the eremitic community and the cenobitic. The eremite lived alone as a hermit away from other people, completely committed to the ascetic life. Those of the eremitic community lived in individual dwellings near other hermits. Those of the cenobitic community lived together in a monastery and their ascetic living was guided by a head monk.

There are two Black men and one Black woman who deserve the credit as founders of Christian monasticism. First is St. Antony, who was the first Christian known to live as a eremite and to form a eremitic community. The second is Pachomius, who instituted the cenobitic form of monastic living that became known as Pachomian Monasticism. Mary, the sister of Pachomius, founded the first nunneries (or convents) of Christianity.

The contributions of the Christian monasteries of Africa to Christianity cannot be overstated. They set the pace for Christian monasticism throughout the world. They translated and preserved scriptural documents and they provided living examples of lives totally committed to God through Christ.

Antony was born of Christian parents around 250 C.E. in Coma in Middle Egypt. His parents died around 269 C.E., leaving him their wealth and the responsibility as guardian of a younger sister. Several months later, Antony's life was changed when he heard the story of the young wealthy man told by Jesus: "If you wish to be perfect, go sell your possessions, and give the money to the poor, and you will have treasures in heaven; then come, follow me." (Matthew 19:21) Unlike the young man in the story, Antony accepted this challenge to become "perfect." He sold all of his material goods, distributed his property among the people of his town, and gave his money to the poor.[134]

---

[134]Robert T. Meyer. translator. *St. Athanasius The life of St. Anthony*. New York: Newman Press, 1950, p. 3

He placed his sister in the care of the women of his community and moved into the desert to live the ascetic life. Antony learned from other Egyptian men who already were living the ascetic life and applied biblical concepts to this ancient Egyptian practice. He lived a life of prayer, fasting and manual labor. Antony was about 20 years old when he had a friend lock him inside a vault of tombs, bringing him bread and water from time to time. He stayed there for 15 years, learning to resist temptation and being attacked by demons. While there, he received a vision from God telling him that he would always be by his side and that Antony would be world renown.

Antony then moved to a desert fort at Pispir, Egypt, where he lived for 20 years. This became his "Outer Mountain." There were many people who came to him to receive guidance on how they could live the monastic life. They were inspired by his life of sacrifice, amazed by miracles performed by him and divinely moved by his preaching about the love of Christ. He became the leader and teacher of those who came to live the monastic life at Pispir. When he wanted to be alone, he traveled further into the desert toward the Red Sea, where he found a spring and date palms. This was his "Inner Mountain." He grew a small garden there and this was his place of personal prayer and meditation.

He presented teachings on the vocation of the monk, the power of prayer over Satan, gifts of the spirit and discerning good and evil spirits.[135] He strongly opposed Arianism and denounced their views. He led a group of monks to Alexandria to minister to persecuted Christians and hoped that he would be martyred while there. Upon returning from Alexandria he increased his acts of self-sacrifice by fasting more, giving up bathing and by wearing a hair shirt (worn with the animal hairs against the skin to cause discomfort).

He continued to grow in fame. In addition to providing counsel to fellow African Christians, he also counseled Emperor Constantine and two of his sons.[136] As he reached the end of his life, he finally retreated to his "Inner Mountain" and died in 356 C.E. at the age of 105. His fame spread further throughout the world after his death, through an autobiography on his life written by Athanasius, the Bishop of Alexandria.

---

[135]Ibid., p. 5.

[136]Kenneth Scott Latourette. *A History of Christianity, Vol.I.* New York: Harper & Row, Publishers, 1975, p. 226.

Pachomius was born around 292 C.E. at Sne (or Isna) in Upper Egypt. In 312 C.E. he was conscripted into the Roman army and taken to Thebes where he and the other conscripts were held in prison. While imprisoned, he appreciated the kindness showed to him by the Christians who brought them provisions. When he was released from prison around 313 C.E. he became a Christian and was baptized by an eremite named Palomen. He remained a student of Palomen until he received a vision, which led him and several other disciples of Palomen to establish their own community near Ahkmim. Pachomius attracted many eremites to their community and began to guide their spiritual journeys. He scheduled their daily lives, prescribing times for sleep, prayer, eating and work.[137]

For anyone seeking to join the Pachomian monastery, they had to complete a probationary period before being given a habit (clothing worn by the monk) and being accepted as a member of the community.

Pachomius founded more than 11 monasteries in Upper Egypt. Each monastery held as many as 300 monks and was surrounded by a wall. There were houses within the walls, and each house had individual cells for 20 to 40 monks. Each house also had a church, meeting room, kitchen, dining room, library and infirmary.[138] Daily life in a Pachomian monastery consisted of daily prayer, Eucharist (taking of bread and wine to symbolize the body and blood of Christ) twice a week, sleeping in a sitting position, memorization of scriptures, manual labor, two meals a day (no meats or wine were allowed), community fasting twice a week, chastity and poverty.

Pachomius' sister, Mary, founded the first Christian nunnery or convent. Though they were an official part of Pachomian monasticism, the men and women were kept separate.

Pachomius died in a plague in 346 C.E. Despite internal conflicts about leadership of the monasteries, the Pachomian monastic form spread throughout the world. There is no doubt that the monks and nuns of the world owe a debt of respect to Antony, Pachomius and Mary.

---

[137]Jill Kamil. *Coptic Egypt History and Guide*. Cairo: The American University in Cairo Press, 1987, pp. 39-40.

[138]Latourette, *A History of Christianity Vol.I*, p. 227.

It's also important to acknowledge the impact on monasticism by Augustine of Hippo. Though he did not personally establish a monastic order (nor did he seek to), one was established based on his sermons, lifestyle and writings regarding the ordering of monastic life in Hippo. His *Letter 211* to the nuns at the monastery was a source especially important to the ministry of Benedict (founder of the Benedictine Order).

The monasteries of Egypt were well known and respected throughout the world. According to Jill Kamil, author of *Coptic Egypt History and Guide*, "Pilgrims came from all over the Christian world to visit the monasteries of Egypt." Ten thousand monks met at Arsinoe in the Fayoum at the end of the 5th Century.

The spread of monasticism to Europe was influenced, and sometimes initiated, by Egyptian monks. According to Dr. Thomas C. Oden, director of the Center for Early African Christianity, "The course of the monastic movement in Africa was well-formed prior to the time of Benedict of Nursia (480-550), the key figure of European monasticism. After Augustine [of Hippo] it would flow into Benedictine and other orders to influence the whole of Medieval culture. In due time the African monastic fruits begun by Antony, Pachomius and Augustine came to flower in Italy and France, and all the way from Ireland and Northumberland to Dalmatia."[139] The spread of Christianity to England and Ireland was initiated by Egyptian monks. In fact, Irish Christianity is regarded as "the child of the Egyptian Church."[140]

At the beginning of the 6th Century, there were more than 10,000 monks and 20,000 nuns.[141] The nine Coptic monasteries that survive to today have provided leadership for the Coptic church. Of the 117 Patriarchs of the Coptic Church between 412 C.E. and 1988, 93 were monks. Today, all Coptic patriarchs and bishops are chosen from the monasteries.[142]

---

[139]Oden, Thomas C. *How Africa Shaped the Christian Mind*. Downer Grove, IL: IVP Books, 2007, p. 52.

[140]Meinardus, Otto F.A. *Christian Egypt Ancient and Modern*. Cairo: The American University in Cairo, 1977, pp. 23-24.

[141]Kamil, *Coptic Egypt History and Guide*, pp. 47-48.

[142]Watterson, Barbara. *Coptic Egypt*. Edinburgh: Scottish Academic Press, 1988, p. 76.

*Chapter 13*

# PRESERVERS OF THE SCRIPTURES

The Bible is unique in several special ways. Unlike most books, it is comprised of many different books by many different writers. All of the original or primary sources of the biblical books were either destroyed or lost over time. The Bible covers over 2 million (or at least 6000) years of human history. It has been revised into more than100 versions and thousands of languages over the last 500 years. According to Guinness Book of world records, it is the #1 top selling book of all times with over 5 billion sold.

If it is true that all of the writers of the biblical books were Israelites/Jews, then it is true that all of these books were most likely written by Black men. It is unlikely that they were white, yet they are popularly perceived as such.

It is also true that the translating of the original manuscripts was done in Africa. The 39 Old Testament books were first translated and compiled from different Hebrew writings in Alexandria, Egypt. This compilation became known as the *Septuagint*, which is interpreted as "seventy." According to tradition, around 250 B.C.E. 72 Jewish scholars met in Alexandria for 72 days to translate the Pentateuch (the first five books of the Old Testament) into Koine, a vernacular of Greek. However, it took more than 200 years for Alexandrian Jews to translate all of the Hebrew writings.[143] The 27 New Testament books were first listed in today's familiar order (Matthew to Revelation) by Athanasius, Bishop of Alexandria, in 367 C.E.

Between 375 and 395 C.E., the New Testament books were translated into the Coptic language (common in Egypt) by Egyptian monks. This language was developed by transliterating Egyptian sounds into the Greek alphabet and by adding seven Egyptian alphabets for sounds not represented by Greek letters. The Coptic translations of the New Testament were written specifically for the large Egyptian Christian population. The colloquial form of this translation made the New Testament accessible to the Egyptian masses that did not read Koine (Greek).

---

[143]Harris, Stephen L. *Understanding the Bible*. Palo Alto, CA: Mayfield Publishing Company, 1980, pp. 7-8.

It is interesting to note the translators chose the word *Nute* to identify God. Nute is the Coptic form of Netcherw. The Netcherw, from which the word nature is derived, represents the many aspects of the one Supreme God in Egyptian Cosmogony.[144]

Scriptural manuscripts were widely distributed and discussed among early Christians in North Africa. During certain periods of Roman persecution, scriptural documents were confiscated and destroyed. One of the most severe instances was around 300 C.E. during the persecution of Emperor Diocletian. Some presbyters turned over their manuscripts to save their lives. After the persecution ended, and Constantine declared toleration of Christianity, those church leaders who turned over the sacred books were viewed as traitors. This sparked the Donatist controversy, a movement led by Donatus, Bishop of Carthage, to declare the religious authority of the traitors as invalid.[145]

Millions of Greek, Coptic and Arabic papyrus documents were destroyed by excavations of Egypt.[146] Despite the destruction of scriptural and other Christian literature from Africa, many important documents have survived.

The three oldest existing biblical manuscripts are the *Vatican Manuscript*, named so because it is kept at the Vatican; the *Sinaitic Manuscript*, which was originally found in a monastery on Mt Sinai; and the *Alexandrian Manuscript*, which was written in Alexandria.[147] British scholars B.F. Westcott and F.H. Hort developed a system to classify all biblical manuscripts. Four families of classification are produced from this system. They are the *Western Text*, the *Alexandrian Text*, the *Neutral Text* and the *Koine or Byzantine Text*. The manuscripts of the Alexandrian Text

---

[144]Latourette, Kenneth Scott. *A History of Christianity Vol.I*. New York: Harper & Row Publishers, 1975, pp. 250-251 and Kamil, *Coptic Egypt History and Guide*, pp. 46-47.

[145]Bainton, Roland H. *Early Christianity*. Florida: Robert E. Krieger Publishing, 1984, pp. 64-65.

[146]Pearson, Birger A. and James E. Goering, Editors. *The Roots of Egyptian Christianity*. Philadelphia: Fortress Press, 1986, p. 44.

[147]Lightfoot, Neil R. *How We Got the Bible*. Grand Rapids: Baker Book House, 1963, pp. 30-34.

family (also called the Egyptian Text-Type) are the oldest of biblical manuscripts in existence. They date from the 2nd Century C.E. to the 4th Century C.E.

The Vatican Manuscript (classified as Codex Vaticanus or Codex B), the Sinaitic Manuscript (classified as Codex Sinaiticus or Codex Aleph) and the Alexandrian Manuscript (classified as Codex Alexandrinus or Codex A) are all categorized into the Alexandrian Text family. Manuscripts classified in the Alexandrian Text family were widely quoted by such Alexandrian church fathers as Clement, Origen and Cyril. It is reasonable to hypothesize that the popular use of these types of manuscripts among African church leaders indicates that they originated in Alexandria.[148]

Since 1876 there have been more than forty major works published on Coptic documents that have been found in Egypt. The most significant find was in 1945, when 52 papyrus texts were found near Nag Hammadi in the Egyptian desert. They are called the *Nag Hammadi Library*.

These Coptic writings date back to the 2nd and maybe the 1st Century. They are original Coptic translations (though not the original texts) of various gnostic gospels and other secret texts. It is likely they were hidden because they were condemned as heretical by Athanasius in 367 C.E. Previously unknown gospels included in the Nag Hammadi Library are the *Gospel of Thomas*, the *Gospel of Truth* and the *Gospel of the Egyptians*.[149]

---

[148]Koester, Helmut. *History and Literature of Early Christianity*. New York: Walter de Gruyter, 1987, pp. 17-18.

[149]Pagels, *The Gnostic Gospels*, p. 14.

*Chapter 14*

# AFRICAN MARTYRS FOR CHRIST

Throughout its first 300 years, Christianity was not an authorized religion of the Roman government. The persecuting of Christians took many different forms. Some emperors expressed little concern about the Christians, while others used deadly force to persecute them. These periods of persecution were often sparked by lies told about Christian beliefs and practices. They also resulted from the government's attempts to maintain consistency and uniformity of beliefs throughout the empire, or to appease the Roman gods.

It was Emperor Trajan (98-117 C.E.) who established a policy toward Christians that guided the government's enforcement of Roman law for his successors. He ruled that government would not seek out Christians to be prosecuted but would investigate accusations against Christians. It's important to point out that Christians were not convicted for being Christians, they were charged and convicted for not honoring the emperor's status as divine, or for not worshiping Roman gods.

An accused Christian would be required to complete an act of worship for the emperor or a deity. If they did not they were imprisoned. If they continued to resist, they would be tortured. If they still refused to submit they would be put to death for their obstinacy. In most cases, the persecutions were not widespread throughout the Roman Empire.

Just as some emperors and government officials were aggressive in their brutality toward non-conforming Christians, so were many Christians just as determined and eager to sacrifice themselves for the cause of Christ.

This outlines periods of persecution from Nero to Galairus:

| **Emperor** | **Years** | **Type of Persecution** |
|---|---|---|
| **Nero** | 54-68 C.E. | Torture and death |

*(Galba, Otho, Vitellius, Vespasian, and Titus served from 68 to 81 C.E. and did not persecution)*

| | | |
|---|---|---|
| **Domitian** | 81-96 C.E. | Torture and death |

*(Nerva served from 96-98 C.E. and did not persecute)*

**Trajan** 98-117 C.E. Torture and death
*(Hadrian, and Antoninus Pius served from 117-161 and basically left the Christians alone unless charges were brought)*

**Marcus Aurelius** 161-180 C.E. Torture and death
*(Lucius Verus, Commodus, Pertinax, and Didius Julianus served from 161-193 C.E. and basically left the Christians alone)*

**Septimus Severus** 193-211 C.E. Torture and death
*(Caracalia, Geta, Macrinus and Diadumenian, Elagalabus, and Severus Alexander served from 211-235 C.E. and did not persecute)*

**Maximus I** 235-238 C.E. Torture and death
*(Gordian I, Gordius II, Pupienus, Balbinus, Godian III, and Philip I, served from 238-249 C.E. and did not persecute)*

**Trajan Decius** 249-251 C.E. Torture and death widely
*(Hostilians, Trebonianus Galius and Volusianus, and Aemilian served from 251-253 C.E. and did not persecute)*

**Valerian** 253-260 C.E. Torture and death
*(Gallienus, Claudius Gothicus, and Quintilius served from 260-270 C.E. and did not persecute)*

**Aurelian** 270–275 C.E. Some torture and death
*(Tacitus, Florian, Probus, Calus, Numerian, and Carinus served from 275-285 C.E. and did not lead persecutions)*
Catholic

**Diocletian/Galerius** 284-311 C.E. Torture and death

During the 1st Century, most of the original apostles were violently put to death. Bartholomew's skin was ripped from his body, James (the son of Zebedee) and Paul were beheaded, and Philip and Peter were crucified. Nero used Christians as human torches. Many more Christians were put to death throughout the Roman Empire.

The reports of bravery among African martyrs are quite inspiring. One such account is of the Scillitan Martyrs. They were 12 Numidians who were executed in Carthage on July 17, 180 C.E.

In 202 C.E. Emperor Septimius Severus issued an edict forbidding Christians and Jews from making new converts. Violators were subject to banishment, forced labor in the imperial mines, torture or death. Many Christians chose death. Among the great martyrs of the early church was a 22-year-old African woman named Perpetua. In 203 C.E. her courage was proven when she personally directed the weapon of an inexperienced executioner against her own breast. The story of her bravery spread throughout North Africa.[150]

Many African martyrs were produced from this period of persecution. Several students of the Catechetical school were put to death, including Plutarch; Serenus (who was burned to death); Heraclides and Hero (a derivative of the name Heru or Horus), both of whom were beheaded; another Serenus, who was tortured to death with an axe; and Herais, a woman burned to death.

Another African woman who gained fame for her courage in defending her faith was Potamiaena. Eusebius described her as having "chastity and virginity, which were beyond reproach." in 205 C.E. the Roman judge Aquila subjected Potamiaena's whole body to painful agony, and also threatened to allow the gladiators to rape her. She was brutally tortured before she and her mother (Marcella) were burned to death. Many Alexandrian Christians claimed they had visions of Potamiaena before they openly affirmed their conversion to Christianity and were put to death.[151]

In 250 C.E. the Emperor Decius initiated another period of persecution. Dionysius, Bishop of Alexandria, reported of many Africans put to death in Alexandria before the official edict was given by Decius. He wrote about an

---

[150]J.C. degraft-Johnson. *African Glory*. Baltimore: Black Classic Press, 1954, pp. 32,40-41.

[151]G.A. Williamson, translator. *Eusebius: The History of the Church from Christ to Constantine*. Minneapolis: Augsburg Publishing House, 1965, pp. 244-246.

old man named Metras, who was brutally clubbed before pointed reeds were driven into his eyes and face. He was then stoned to death. Also killed was a woman named Quinta, who was dragged through the streets and then stoned to death. In the case of an elder Christian woman named Apollonia, who refused to recite "heathen incantations," and her persecutors knocked out all of her teeth. While still being tortured, she asked for breathing space. When they released her, she jumped to her death into a raging fire that had been prepared for her.

When the official edict came, many other Africans were put to death. Those who suffered in this wave of persecutions, to name a few, included a Libyan named Macar, who was burned to death; and four women, Ammonarion, Mercuria, Dionysia, and another Ammonarion, all of whom died by the sword.[152] Some Christians hid themselves in the desert and mountains and many died from starvation or wild beasts.

The final and most severe period of persecution came in 304 C.E. and was instigated by Galarius and issued by Maximian, who were joint Emperors with Diocletian. Eusebius reports of Africans enduring outrageous agonies in Thebaid. These Christians were "torn to bits from head to foot with potsherds like claws."[153] Women were tortured by being hoisted in the air naked with a rope tied to only one foot. For years, many men, women and children were put to death. In 311 C.E. the persecutions were ended by Galarius, who was dying of a painful disease.

These Black men and women suffered brutal persecution without resorting to violence to save themselves. They perfected the concept of non-violent resistance more than 1,600 years before Mohandas Gandhi and Dr. Martin Luther King, Jr. popularized the concept in the 20$^{th}$ Century.

---

[152]Ibid., pp. 275-278.

[153]David Ayerst and A.S.T. Fisher. *Records of Christianity*. Oxford: Basil Blackwell, p. 137.

*Chapter 15*

# THE 1st GREAT SCHISM of CHRISTIANITY

During its first 500 years of the Church, the leaders tried to establish one universal church with a consistent doctrine. The word "catholic" means universal and was used to describe this concept of a unified Christian church. This consistency was never reached. In fact, the conflicts grew.

There were many different theological, social and political issues that contributed to the splitting of the Church. Some of the factors included the attempts of Bishops of Rome and Alexandria to gain supremacy over other sees; factionalism produced from diverse theological perspectives; and political manipulation of the Church by imperial authorities.

Though there were many factors that led to the split, the conflicts produced by the Arian controversy were the major cause. It started around 324 C.E. in Alexandria when an Egyptian presbyter named Arius conflicted with Alexander, Bishop of Alexandria, regarding the teachings of Origen on the nature of Christ. Alexander's successor, Athanasius, became the champion in confronting Arius' views.

Origen taught of the "eternal, timeless generation" of the Son of God, but he made the Son (Jesus) subordinate to the Father (God). Arius supported the idea of a subordinate relationship and rejected the concept of an eternal generation. He stated that a "generation" cannot be "timeless." Arius asserted that there was a point in time when the generation of Christ started, giving him a point of beginning. He taught that Jesus was the "first born" of all creation, God's agent in the creation of all else and subject to change because he was a created being. This description of the Son is identical to the description of Amen in Egyptian mythology and may be one reason why it was rejected by many as heretical.

Athanasius argued that if the Son is not eternally the Son, then neither is the Father's role eternal. If the Son is subject to change, there is no sure ground for the doctrine of eternal salvation. In 325 C.E. the Council of Nicea declared Arianism as heretical and concluded that "the Son is one being, or essence, or substance with the Father, and those that say that he was made out of nothing, or that his being is different from that of the Father are anathema."[154]

The issue did not end. It smoldered and eventually grew into a raging controversy that completed the splitting of the Church. The decision reached at the Council of Nicea was reversed at an Arian-controlled council meeting held in Tyre in 335 C.E. In 356 C.E. opponents of Arianism were forced into exile by the Emperor Constantius, who was an Arian. This period of exile ended in 361 C.E. and another short period of exile began in 364 C.E.

In 381 C.E. Emperor Theodosius I, a strict Christian orthodox against Arianism, held a council meeting at Constantinople. This council reaffirmed the Nicene Creed and officially added the Holy Spirit to the Father and Son to complete the trinity of three uncreated aspects of the one God. They also recognized the See of Alexandria as subordinate to the See of Constantinople, which was made a major center for Christianity by Constantine.[155] This council meeting displeased many African church leaders and helped to further strengthen a nationalistic fervor that always existed among many of the African church leaders.

The next stage of the controversy involved Nestorius, Bishop of Constantinople, and Cyril, Bishop of Alexandria. In 430 C.E. Cyril held a local council in Alexandria to challenge Nestorius' teachings that "the Virgin" Mary was the *Christotokos* (Christ-bearing or Mother of Christ), conflicting with a more popular belief in Mary as the *Theotokos* (God-

---

154Roland H. Bainton. *Early Christianity.* Florida: Robert E. Krieger Publishing, 1984, p. 68.

155Kenneth Scott Latourette. *A History of Christianity Vol. I.* New York: Harper & Row, Publishers, 1975, p. 164 and Barbara Watterson. *Coptic Egypt.* Edinburgh: Scottish Academic Press, 1988, p. 42.

bearing or Mother of God).

A general council of all church bishops was called in 431 C.E. by Emperor Theodosius II and held in Ephesus. Cyril had the support of the Bishops of African sees and Ephesus. Supporters of Nestorius arrived several days late. The supporters of Cyril seized this opportunity to condemn and depose Nestorius. When supporters of Nestorius arrived, they protested the council's decision. The matter was presented to the Emperor, who temporarily deposed Cyril and Nestorius. It was decided in 433 C.E. that Jesus was "true God and true man, consisting of a reasonable soul and a body."[156] Nestorius remained exiled in Egypt until his death in 444.

In 449 C.E. a monk named Eutyches from Constantinople challenged the decision reached in 433. He denounced the decision as Nestorianism. In 449 Theodosius II called the bishops to a council meeting in Ephesus. Eutyches taught that before the union (incarnation), there were two natures, divine and human. These natures became one, after the union. Eutyches was opposed by Flavian, Bishop of Constantinople, and supported by Dioscurus, Bishop of Alexandria. The council upheld the opinion of Eutyches. Dioscurus, who presided over the council, excommunicated the Bishops of Rome, Antioch and Constantinople. The losers in this conflict called the meeting the "Robber Council." However, this victory was short lived.

In 451 C.E. Marcian, the successor to Theodosius II, called the bishops to another council meeting in Chalcedon. This meeting was the last major council of the Church before the split. This council concluded that the son was perfect in "Godhead" and perfect in "manhood," truly God and truly man. This acknowledgement of two natures is called the Diphysite view. The council further concluded that the Son and Father were of the same substance (*homoousion*); that the son was without sin and the only begotten of the Father; and that the Virgin was the Mother of God (*Theotokos*).

Eutyches was denounced as a heretic and Dioscurus was deposed and excommunicated. This council also established a church hierarchy,

---

156 Latourette, *A History of Christianity Vol.I*, p. 168.

recognizing Rome as the superior see and Constantinople as the second in authority.

The decisions reached at Chalcedon produced a fatal split between the eastern sees of Alexandria, Antioch and Jerusalem, from the western sees of Rome and Constantinople. Throughout the next 200 years, the Egyptian church developed its own independent structure separate from the politically enforced "Catholic" church. The term "Coptic" is popularly used to distinguish this branch of Christianity. "Coptic" or "Copt" is derived from the Greek *Aiguptious*, a word used to identify the Egyptians, separate from the Greeks and other nationalities living in Egypt.

The Coptic Church maintained a Monophysite view, recognizing the Father and Son as one nature. The Monophysite doctrine had some supporters from time to time in other parts of the Christian world, but it was recognized as a belief consistent with Egyptian nationalism. Those few Egyptians who were Diphysites were regarded as *Melkites* or the king's Christians. They composed the membership of the Orthodox Church in Egypt. The majority of Egyptian Christians belonged to the Coptic Church.

Attempts to suppress the Coptic Church continued from 451 C.E. until the rise of Islam in 642. Islam presented a serious challenge to Coptic Christianity. Many Copts accepted Islam, while others were forced south into Ethiopia. Athanasius appointed Frumentarius, a Syrian, as the first bishop of the church in Ethiopia in the 4th Century. This church provided a place of refuge for Coptic Christians.

The Coptic and Orthodox Christians who remained in Egypt were forced to pay large taxes to the Islamic rulers and they had to wear distinctive clothing to make them easy to recognize. Under Islamic rule, the Christians were not allowed to build new churches, ring the church bell, display the cross in public or ride a horse. There was no pressure to conform to a specific form of Christianity because they were all given the same rights.[157] In 705

---

[157]Leo Donald Davis. *The First Seven Ecumenical Councils (325-787)*. Wilmington: Michael Glazier, Inc., 1987, p. 269.

C.E. the Copts were forced to use the Arabic language instead of the Coptic language.

Towards the end of the 10th Century, a new dynasty of Moslem rulers, the Fatimids, gained power in Egypt from the Addasid, Caliph of Baghdad. In the beginning, they eased restrictions against the Christians, some of whom reached high positions in government. However, around 1200 C.E., the Caliph Hakim began a period of Christian persecution. Following generations brought varying degrees of persecution.[158] In the 12th Century, most Egyptian and Ethiopian Christians belonged to the Coptic Church.

Islam has remained as the dominant religion in Egypt, as about 90 percent of the Egyptians are Moslems. At the end of the 19th Century, there were approximately 500,000 Coptic Christians. Today there are more than 4.7 million Coptic Christians, most living in Ethiopia. Many of their original customs have survived, such as the ceremonial use of the Coptic language; their calendar, based of the flow of the Nile River; circumcision; and burial customs.[159]

The growth of Coptic Christianity beyond Africa is not clear. The Rastafarians of Jamaica were influenced by the Ethiopian Coptic Faith, a church formed in Jamaica by Joseph N. Hibbert. There are several Coptic churches in America. In the 1950s Prophet Melchizedek (Louis Cicero Patterson) founded the Universal Prayer House and Training School, on the south side of Chicago, IL. After his death, his work was continued by Prophet Peter (Eddie Banks), who founded the True Temple of Solomon, which continues to be an active Coptic church in Chicago, and his ministry ultimately produced 10 Coptic churches in America. The migration of Coptic Christians throughout the world and increased awareness of Kemitic (Egyptian) beliefs, may cause an increased interest in Coptic Christianity.

---

[158]Latourette, *A History of Christianity Vol.I*, pp. 586-587.

[159]Kenneth Scott Latourette. *The History of the Expansion of Christianity*. New York: Harper & Brothers, 1944.

The supremacy of the Roman Catholic Church was not easily attained. Its contributions to early Christianity were few. The popular perception is that it began with the Apostle Peter as its first pope and remained as the superior see from the 1st Century. However, the truth is its early Christian community was very small. The spread of Christianity began with the Jewish communities of the empire. The earliest record of a Jewish community in Rome dates back to 139 B.C.E.[160] At the same time, there were more than a million Jews living in Egypt. In the 1st Century there were only 40,000 to 50,000 Jews living in Rome. There were also times when the Emperor expelled Jews from Rome in 19 C.E. and in 49 C.E. These expulsions decreased the Jewish population there.[161]

Regarding claims that the Apostle Peter founded the See of Rome, there is no evidence that this ever happened. In fact, this belief in Peter as the first Roman Pope began in the 3rd Century and was used as justification for claiming religious supremacy over the entire Christian world. It is likely that he was martyred in Rome, where he was buried near Vatican Hill around 64 C.E. According to Raymond E. Brown, co-author of *Antioch & Rome New Testament Cradles of Catholic Christianity*, "We have no knowledge at all of when he [Peter] came to Rome and what he did there before he was martyred. Certainly, he was not the original missionary who brought Christianity to Rome (and therefore not the founder of the church of Rome in that sense). There is no serious proof that he was the bishop (or local ecclesiastical officer) of the Roman church, a claim not made until the 3rd Century."[162]

The earliest record of Christians in Rome comes from Tacitus, who states that the Christians were blamed for a fire that burned most of Rome in 64 C.E. Tacitus reports that Emperor Nero had these Christians attacked by

---

[160]Raymond E. Brown and John P. Meier. *Antioch & Rome New Testament Cradles of Catholic Christianity*. New York: Paulist Press, 1982, p. 93.

[161]Ibid., pp. 94-95.

[162]Ibid., p. 98.

dogs and used them as human torches.[163] The presence of a distinct community of Christians in Rome in 64 C.E. and references to the Roman Church made by Paul indicate that the church began around 50 C.E.

The term "catholic," which means universal, was used collectively to describe all of the sees. It is now generally used to describe all of the churches founded under the authority of the Roman Church, headed by its bishop or pope. It was Pope Leo I (440 to 461 C.E.) who popularized the belief that the Roman pope solely held the authority of Christ. He argued that this authority was first given to Peter and then passed on through the bishops of the Roman church. Later popes also used a document, then believed to be authentic, called the *Donations of Constantine*. The Roman church claimed that Emperor Constantine donated his palace in Rome, the city of Rome and all of Italy to the church to express his gratitude to Sylvester I, the Bishop of Rome, who converted, baptized and healed him of leprosy. This document was later identified as a forgery.[164]

The claims of superiority made by the Roman church resulted in another split that produced the Greek Orthodox or Eastern Orthodox Church in the 13th Century. Since the Council of Chalcedon, this eastern (Constantinople) branch of the church grew distant from the western (Roman) branch. Many factors contributed to this split; factors that don't directly relate to the purpose of this book.

The growth of the Roman Catholic Church throughout the world resulted from its connections to various imperial or political powers. Most recently, it has suffered financial difficulties; controversies about sexual abuse; theological controversies (e.g. the ordination of women, celibacy of the priest and marriage of priest); a decline in parishioners; and a serious decline in recruitment of new priests.

---

[163]Watterson, *Coptic Egypt*, p. 19.

[164]Patrick Granfield. *The Papacy in Transition*. Dublin: Gill and MacMillan, 1981, p. 5 (footnote 8).

*Chapter 16*

# HOW CHRISTIANITY WAS COLORED WHITE

Friedrich Nietzsche, a 19th Century German philologist and philosopher, who was quite critical of Christianity, wrote the following about history:

> *History is necessary to the man of conservative and reverent nature, who looks back to the origins of his existence with love and trust; through it he gives thanks for life. He is careful to preserve what survives from ancient days, and will reproduce the conditions of his own upbringing for those who come after him; thus he does life a service. The possessions of his ancestors' furniture changes its meaning in his soul; for his soul is rather possessed by it....The history of his town becomes the history of himself; he looks on the walls, the turreted gates, the town council, the fair, as an illustrated diary of his youth, and sees himself in it all.*[165]

It was this approach to history that guided the later European church in its recreation of Christian/biblical history. The distorting of history and creating of white biblical characters was done to allow the European the opportunity to see himself in his Christian heritage, as himself. The exclusion of true Black images from the Europeans' interpretation of biblical events was a by-product of their attempts to see themselves in a history that seldom included their race.

The racism that infects the minds of the present generations did not exist in early Christianity. This present form of racism is represented by the belief that people of the lightest hues are superior to people of the darkest hues. This form of racism is represented by the distorting of history to create a false

---

[165]Friedrich Nietzsche. *The Use and Abuse of History*. New York: The Liberal Arts Press, 1949, p. 25.

past to justify a false present, which is inevitably leading to more confusion and hatred in the future.

To recreate historical figures in ways that alter the facts of the past cannot be called history. It falls into the category of mis-information. Biblical history has been altered in many different ways for many different reasons. To embellish and hyperbolize a historical event in order to make clear the lessons to be learned from past events is often harmless and can be a good thing. To distort historical events to create an advantage for one group of people, while creating disadvantage for another group, is evil, careless, reckless and mean-spirited.

Sometime within the last 2,000 years the motives of European historians changed from trying to include themselves in the biblical story to trying to completely exclude Black (or dark hued) people from the biblical story. This process of exclusion directly contributed to the formation of the form of racism that identified Black people as inhuman. This process of exclusion directly contributed to the brutal slave trade and colonialism that has almost destroyed Black people. This process of exclusion directly contributes to the present form of racism that gives whites a sense of superiority and Blacks a sense of inferiority.

The use of white images as biblical/Christian characters probably started late in the 4th Century when Christianity became the official religion of the Roman Empire. The imperial Roman commitment to Christianity was based on the need for the empire to have a uniform religious belief system. Christianity was not chosen as the state religion because of Constantine's belief in Jesus. He continued to worship other gods long after his "conversion" to Christianity. By combining some pagan beliefs with Christian beliefs, the Roman government attempted to make Christianity acceptable to the masses of people under Roman rule.

For this reason, Isis and Horus were equated with Mary and Jesus; Serapis, Osiris and Horus were equated with Jesus; and the festivals of Ishtar and Mithra were given Christian imagery and celebrated as Easter and Christmas. The image of Serapis and some white images of Jesus are very similar. Serapis was the creation of Ptolemy I, made around 300 B.C.E. through merging Osiris with Apis, a Memphite god. Worship of Serapis was popular among some people of Alexandria but was widely rejected by Jews and most Egyptians. Walter Williams, author of *The Historical Origin of Christianity*, argued that the Serapis image was used to depict Jesus in the 4th Century.[166] It is possible that the Serapis image was used to represent Jesus among some Roman Christians, but not among Coptic Christians.

Most of the portraits, paintings, carvings and sculptures of biblical figures were produced more than 400 years after biblical times by European artists. There is a suspicious lack of archaeological evidence depicting Jews and Palestinians who lived during the early Christian era. Most of the few existing images depict them as Black or dark-skinned people. I traveled to Israel in 2006 and visited many of the tradition sites of Christianity. I also visited a museum at Tel Megiddo. In all cases, there were almost no images of the people. The few I saw did not depict them as white.

From the 14th to 16th Centuries, a period of Christian art produced many white images of biblical characters. Some of the artists involved in this period were Fra Angelico (1387-1455), Giotto (1267-1337), Robert Campin (1375-1444), Donatello (1386-1466), Filippo Lippi (1406-1469), and Annibale Carracci (1560-1609). The most notable artists of this period were Leonardo da Vinci (1452-1519), Raphael (1483-1520) and Michelangelo (1475-1564).

In 1495 Duke Lodovico Sforza commissioned Da Vinci to paint *The Last Supper*. The controversies surrounding the origin and assumed subliminal messages of his paintings of biblical images (popularized by *The Da Vinci Code* by Dan Brown) is fascinating, but not historically substantive. Da Vinci's motives for painting biblical persons the ways he did certainly represent his unique style, but also the artistic perceptions of his day. Other

---

[166]Walter Williams. *The Historical Origin of Christianity*. Chicago: Maathian Press, Inc. 1992, p. iii and Jill Kamil. *Coptic Egypt History and Guide*. Cairo: The American University in Cairo Press, 1987, p. 20.

paintings of biblical people by Da Vinci include *The Virgin of the Rocks, The Virgin and Child with Saint Anne and Saint John the Baptist,* and *Virgin Mary, from the Annunciation.*

In 1508 Raphael and Michelangelo were commissioned by Pope Julius II to paint biblical images. Works produced by Raphael include *Christ Bearing the Cross*, *Madonna*, *Holy Family*, and *The Marriage of Joseph and the Virgin*. He also painted frescoes in the Vatican, such as *The Fall of Adam* and *Solomon's Judgement*.

The paintings by Michelangelo on the ceilings of the Sistine Chapel are regarded as a masterpiece of decorative design. This series includes the *History of Moses*, the *Life of Christ*, the *Creation*, the *History of Noah*, the *Prophets* and the *Last Judgement*.

These images were later printed in large, illustrated King James versions of the Bible and passed on by families, from one generation to the next. For many people, these were the earliest biblical images to which they were introduced. These images are also recreated in paintings, mosaics and stained glass in thousands of churches throughout the world. Many Christians believe that biblical people spoke in an old English dialect, using "thee," "art," "ye," "lo" and "thou." This was not the way that the people of Bible spoke. The ancient Israelites spoke Hebrew, and the 1st Century Jews spoke Aramaic.

Most impressive and popular are the motion pictures of biblical events. Since the late 1950s, new films are made each year, depicting the biblical figures as white. Billions of people have been exposed to these images that, while blatantly glorifying the biblical characters, with subtlety they glorify the race of the white actors playing the biblical characters.

A major contributing factor to the confusion regarding the race of the ancient and 1st Century Israelites is the fact that many Jews of today are white. It is logical to conclude that if the majority of those people who are called Jews today are white, then their ancestors were white. If these white Jews are the descendants of the ancient Israelites, then the ancient Israelites were white. However, the ancient Israelites were not white, they were Black. As Black people, their genetic dominance (based on Mendel's Law) should produce Black or dark hued descendants. In order for the ancient Jews to have become a white people, they would have had to undergo a genetic mutation. This was not the case.

Though many of modern Jews are actual Jews (religiously), they are not Semitic descendants of the ancient Israelites. The two main types of modern Jews are Ashkenazi and Sephardim. Roughly 80 percent of those people who identify themselves as Jews are Ashkenazi Jews. The word "Sephardim" comes from the Hebrew word *Sepharad*, which means Spain, and is used to identify the Jews who descended from ancestors that lived in Spain until the 15th Century. In the 1960s, there were about 500,000 Sephardim Jews. Today there are 2.2 million Sephardim Jews.

The actual meaning of Ashkenazi is unclear. The Hebrew word Ashkenaz was used to refer to Germany. The Bible identifies Ashkenaz as the name for a grandson of Japheth. Ashkenazi is used in general to identify those Jews who descended from ancestors who lived in Eastern Europe. There were about 11 million Ashkenazi Jews during the 1960s.[167] Today the number of Ashkanazi Jews remains unchanged from 60 years ago, at an estimated 10 to 11 million.

It is now believed by many that Ashkenazi Jewry originated with a Turkish people called the Khazars. The Khazar Empire accepted Judaism as the state religion, the same as Rome chose Christianity. In 740 C.E. the Khazars chose Judaism for the sake of neutrality. The choice of Judaism allowed them to maintain their sovereignty without choosing Christianity or Islam as their official religion. Either religion would have made them subject to an established religious hierarchy. Judaism had no religious or political hierarchy but was the foundation from which the other two religions came.[168]

Recent DNA studies have revealed opposing views regarding the genetic

---

[167] Arthur Koestler. *The Thirteenth Tribe*. London: Hutchinson & Co. Publishers, 1976, p. 181.

[168] Ibid., pp. 59-60.

origin of Ashkenazi Jews. Dr. Harry Ostrer, a geneticist at the Albert Einstein College of Medicine and author of *Legacy: A Genetic History of the Jewish People*, argues that there is genetic evidence that the Ashkenazi Jews are descendants of ancient Israel.[169] Ostrer and those who present the same genetic results are rebutted by Dr. Eran Elhaik, who argues that the genetic research verifies that Ashkenazi Jews are the genetic descendants of people of the Caucasus. According to Elhaik, "Ashkenazi Jews' roots lie in the Caucasus — a region at the border of Europe and Asia that lies between the Black and Caspian seas — not in the Middle East. They are descendants, he argues, of the Khazars, a Turkic people who lived in one of the largest medieval states in Eurasia and then migrated to Eastern Europe in the 12th and 13th centuries.[170]

For more than 600 years after their conversion, the Khazars observed Judaism as their official religion. The decline of the Khazar Empire began in 965 C.E. when they were defeated by the Russians. They were allowed to remain independent and continued to practice their Jewish beliefs into the 13th Century. The disappearance of the Khazars from their original homeland (north of the Black Sea, Caucausoid Mountains and Caspian Sea) happened at the same time that Jewish immigrants settled in Germany and Poland.

The vast majority of those people who identify themselves as Jews descended from these Eastern European, or Ashkenazi Jews. They are Jews but, they are not all Hebrews or Israelites by descent. When considering the ancient Israelites (the original 12 tribes), it must be remembered that most of them lost their Israelite heritage long before the 1st Century. After the 1st Century, many Jews became Christians or were later persecuted by the

---

[169]Harry Ostrer, *Legacy: A Genetic History of the Jewish People*. Oxford University Press, 2012.

[170]*Genome Biology and Evolution*, "The Missing Link of Jewish European Ancestry:Contrasting the Rhineland and the Khazarian Hypotheses" by Eran Elhaik, December 14, 2012.

Romans. When Christianity became the official religion of the Roman Empire, the Christians began to persecute Jews and other "pagan" people. During this time, Jews migrated to many different parts of the world. Some even migrated to Khazaria where they probably intermixed with the local population, and participated in the converting of Khazaria, making it the first independent Jewish kingdom since 586 B.C.E.

What's more important for the purposes of this text is the people known as the Falashim Jews (also known as Beta Israel) of Ethiopia. The term Falashim comes from *Falasha*, which is interpreted as migrant, stranger or invader. There are an estimated 150,000 Falashim Jews today. In 1991 Israel began to an immigration campaign and brought 15,000 Falashim to Israel. Since that time, the population of Falashim shifted from Ethiopia to Israel. Today, there are nearly 125,000 Falashim living in Israel.

The temple in Axum where the Ark of the Covenant is believed to be. *Photo by Ernest Augcomfer*

The Falashim claim direct descent from the ancient Israelites and possess ancient Hebrew documents. For more than 2,000 years, there have been rumors that the Ark of the Covenant is in Ethiopia. The Ark was made of precious metals and stones by the Israelites and used to store the tablets of laws made by Moses. It is believed that the Ark is kept in a temple in the ancient city of Axum and is guarded by a secretive order of monks. Graham Hancock, author of *The Sign and the Seal: The Quest for the Lost Ark of the Covenant*, claimed that he located the Ark in Axum. He also revealed the efforts of "a shadowy group of Freemasons" who descended from the Templars (a 12th Century order of Christian knights) in their plot to obtain the Ark.[171]

---

[171] *Biblical Archaeology Review*, "Is the Ark of the Covenant in Ethiopia?"

Studies in genetics pioneered by Dr. Karl Skorecki have yielded a great deal of information about the ethnicity of biblical people. These efforts have already proven that certain DNA sequences are distinctive of the Cohanim, the Jewish priests believed to be the descendants of Aaron. This Cohen Modal Haplotype (CHM) sequence is present in the DNA of Ashkenazi and Sephardic Jews, but not exclusively so. A most surprising example is that of the Lemba tribe of Southern Africa. According to researcher Dr. David Goldstein, of the Laboratory of Evolutionary Genetics, University College, London, whereas the Y chromosomes of nearly 3 to 5 percent of those people generally believed to be Jews (i.e., Ashkenazi and Sephardic) bear the Cohen Modal Haplotype, an astounding 9 percent of the Lemba bear this marker.[172] This chromosomal type being higher among this African (Black) tribe proves that they truly are Jews (more so than the Eastern European Jews of Israel).

We have shared information about Jewish migrations from Israel since the 1st Century to Egypt, Khazaria, Ethiopia, and now Southern Africa. There are African traditions that credit these Jewish migrants with building the Great Zimbabwe ruins, and with possessing a replica of the Ark of the Covenant. There is also research being done of artifacts and traditional claims that may reveal a presence of Jewish migrants as ancestors of the Igbo people of Nigeria.[173]

For nearly 700 years, there have been countless efforts to present the people of the Bible as white. The European Christian world forgot its African heritage in an effort to lift its own race up while brutally subjugating non-European people around the world. The opinion that Christianity is the "white man's religion," and that the Bible was written by "the white man,"

---

by Ephraim Isaac, July/August 1993, pp. 60-63.

[172]*The New York Times*, "DNA Backs a Tribe's Tradition of Early Descent From the Jews" by Nicholas Wade, May 9, 1999.

[173]Israelinternationalnews.com, "Nigeria's 'Igbo Jews' Returning to Their Roots" byRemi Ilona, August 25, 2015. http://www.israelnationalnews.com/News/News.aspx/199864#.VvM2dHoYE0w

became a popular statement of Black cultural nationalists during the 1960s. Despite efforts, sincere or insincere, to "whitewash" Christianity, it is still a religion that began with Black people and is to be shared by all people.

*Chapter 17*

# CHRISTIANITY RECLAIMING its AFRICENTRISM

According to Luke 4:18, Jesus said, "The Spirit of the Lord is upon me, because he has anointed me to bring good news to the poor. He has sent me to proclaim release to the captives and recovery of sight to the blind, to let the oppressed go free, to proclaim the year of the Lord's favor."

Christianity is a religion based on the life, example, and gospel of the Jesus Christ. Jesus spoke of bringing "good news to the poor," but Christian nations have used the gospel to create poverty and hunger in the world.[174] They used their religious authority to justify slavery and colonialism upon which their economic systems are built. A popular saying among many Africans is "When the white man first came, he had his Bible, and we had our land. Now, we have his Bible, and he has our land." In the "name of Jesus," we (as African people) have been robbed of our traditional ways and made to think that African traditions and culture are inferior, uncivilized, or evil. We have been made to think that the Europeans' interpretations of Christianity are superior, civilized and the only way to salvation.[175]

Jesus spoke of bringing release to the captive and setting at liberty the oppressed. Yet Christian nations used their wealth and power to support the enslavement of African people. They used their powers to colonize the world under European rulership. They created more captives and oppressed, rather than creating more liberty and justice. Like a bad little boy that throws a rock

---

[174]James H. Cone. *The Black Theology & Black Power*. New York: The Seabury Press, 1969, pp. 71-73. and Teresa Hayter. *The Creation of World Poverty*. London: Pluto Press, 1990, p. 41.

[175]Marimba Ani. *Yurugu An African-Centered Critique of European Cultural Thought and Behavior*. Trenton, NJ: African World Press, 1994, p. 186.

and then hides his hands, the Eurocentered Christian world is directly responsible for contributing to the poverty, warfare, sickness and death affecting African and aboriginal people, and for taking the lands that they conquered in the name of "manifest destiny." Now they try to make themselves look like the innocent humanitarians and peacemakers of the world.[176] The Christianized European nations of the world claim that they want to create a "New World Order" of peace and prosperity, while they seem to be simultaneously and secretly planning a new era of colonialism and legal slavery.[177]

The world is in serious trouble. There is fear that nuclear war could occur, or that terrorist attacks will escalate. The industries of the world have polluted the land, water and air with toxic chemicals and plastics. The nations of the world are constantly in conflict with each other. For some Christians, their religion has become "the opiate of the people," making them passive and insensitive to the realities around them. In some strangely evil way, the very teachings that can bring us more life and liberty have been used to do the opposite. This must be a false presentation of Christianity, and false religions are the real opiates of the masses. True Christianity is a religion of liberation. The fact that biblical history is African centered by nature is obvious. If the Bible represents the truth of God's relationship with man, then God must have a reason for institutionalizing Christianity through Black people. We insult the wisdom of God when we tell "a little white lie" about the ethnicity of the people of the Bible.

I have personally experienced the reality and power of the Word of God (which is much more than a book), having been brought up in a Christian family, and being a servant of God through the example and salvation offered

---

[176]Hancock, Graham. *Lords of Poverty.* New York: The Atlantic Monthly Press, 1989, pp.7-9.

[177]Eustace Mullins. *The World Order.* Staunton, VA: Ezra Pound Institute of Civilization, 1985, pp. 201-202, 216-217.

through Jesus Christ. My commitment, understanding and submission to the will of God has been multiplied through my learning the culture of my African people. The culture, history and spirituality of Africa complements my Christianity. I am a much better Christian because of my African ways.

The world has been led to believe that anything African is inferior and backwards. The truth is, the very place that the world has been taught to reject is the cradle of humanity, civilization, and the institutionalization of Christianity.

For hundreds of years, Black people have believed Jesus, and all of the biblical figures were white. Many of our Black families have portraits of a "white Jesus" in our homes and churches. Can Christians of all races now accept the reality of Jesus being a Black man, the same as non-Europeans have accepted him as white? Will some Christians reject Jesus because he is Black? Has racism become more important to Christians than their submission to God? Many Christians expect the return of Jesus in his physical form. When this happens, and Jesus returns in his original Black form, will Christians reject their place in God's kingdom because the one sent to lead them is Black?

Christians must accept the fact that historical Christianity is African-centered. Jesus spoke of "recovering of sight to the blind." European-centered Christianity has been used to blind and confuse the masses. When a student learns only half of what the teacher presents, that student is only half informed. If that student becomes an architect, he will have just enough information to design a building that will collapse and kill anyone in the building. The Christian world must accept the African foundation of Christianity and reevaluate Christian history and theology from that bases. Christians must examine the African aspects of Christianity in order to design a life based on the whole truth, and the truth will make us free.

## BIBLIOGRAPHY

Ani, Marimba. *Yurugu An African-Centered Critigue of European Cultural Thought and Behavior*. Trenton: African World Press, Trenton, NJ 1994.

Saint Augustine. *The City of God*. New York: The Modern Library of Random House, 1950.

Ayerst, Davis and A.S.T. Fisher. *Records of Christianity*. Oxford: Basil Blackwell.

Bainton, Roland H. *Early Christianity*. Florida: Robert E. Krieger Publishing, 1984.

Barnstone, Willis, editor. *The Other Bible: Ancient Alternative Scriptures*. San Francisco: Harper Collins Publishers, 1984.

Benz, Ernst. *The Eastern Orthodox Church*. Garden City, NY: Anchor Books of Doubleday & Company, Inc., 1963.

Bernal, Martin. *Black Athena Vol.2*. New Brunswick, NJ: Rutgers University Press, 1991.

*Biblical Archaeology Review*, "Is the Ark of the Covenant in Ethiopia?" by Ephraim Isaac, July/August 1993, pp. 60-63.

Boyd, Paul C. *The African Origin of Christianity Vol.I*. London: Karia Press, 1991.

Brown, Raymond E. and John P. Meier. *Antioch and Rome New Testament Cradles of Catholic Christianity*. New York: Paulist Press, 1982.

Browder, Tony. *Nile Valley Contributions to Civilization*. Washington D.C.: The Institute for Karmic Guidance, 1992.

Budge, E.A. Wallis. *The Book of the Dead*. Sacaucus, NJ: University Books, Inc., 1960.

Clarke, G.W., translator. *The Letters of St. Cyprian of Carthage*. New York: Newmann Press, 1950.

Comay, Joan and Ronald Brownrigg. *Who's Who in the Bible*. New York: Bonanza Books, 1980.

Cone, James H. *Black Theology & Black Power*. New York: The Seabury

Press, 1969.

Conzelmann, Han. *History of Primitive Christianity*. New York: Abingdon Press, 1973.

Copher, Charles B. *Black Biblical Studies*. Chicago: Black Light Fellowship, 1990.

Davis, Leo Donald. *The First Seven Ecumenical Councils (325-787)*. Wilmington, DE: Michael Glazier, Inc., 1987.

Diop, Cheikh Anta. *The African Origin of Civilization*. Westport: Lawrence Hill & Company, 1974.

Diop Chiekh Anta, *Civilization or Barbarism*. Brooklyn: Lawrence Hill Books, 1991.

Diop, Chiekh Anta. *The Cultural Unity of Black Africa*. Chicago: Third World Press, 1978.

Dunston, Bishop Alfred G. Jr. *The Black Man in the Old Testament and its World*. Trenton, NJ: Africa World Press, Inc., 1992.

deGraft-Johnson, J.A. *African Glory*. Baltimore: Black Classic Press, 1954.

Durant, Will. *The Story of Civilization, Part One: Our Oriental Heritage*. New York: Simon and Schuster, 1954.

Felder, Cain Hope, editor. *Stony the Road We Trod*. Minneapolis: Fortress Press, 1991.

Gottwald, Norman K. *All the Kingdoms of the Earth*. New York: Harper and Row Publishers, 1964.

Granfield, Patrick. *The Papacy in Transition*. Dublin: Gill and MacMillan, 1981.

Grant, Robert, M. *Augustus to Constantine*. New York: Harper &. Row, Publishers, 1970.

Grant, Robert M. *Second-Century Christianity*. London: The Trustees of the Society for Promoting Christian Knowledge, 1957.

Griggs, C. Wilfred. *Early Egyptian Christianity from its Origins to 451 C.E.* New York: E.J. Brill, 1990.

Groves, C.P. *The Planting of Christianity in Africa*. London: Lutterworth Press, 1948.

Harney, Martin P. *The Catholic Church Through the Ages.* Boston: Daughters of St. Paul, 1974.

Harris, Joseph E., Editor. *Africa and Africans as Seen by Classical Writers.* Washington D.C.: Howard University Press, 1977.

Harris, Stephen L. *Understanding the Bible*. Palo Alto: Mayfield Publishing Company, 1980.

Hancock, Graham. Lords of Poverty. New York: The Atlantic Monthly Press, 1989.

Hancock, Graham. *The Sign and the Seal: The Quest for the Lost Ark of the Covenant*. New York: Crown, 1992

Hayter, Teresa. *The Creation of World Poverty*. London: Pluto Press, 1990.

Kamil, Jill. *Coptic Egypt History and Guide*. Cairo: The American University in Cairo Press, 1987.

Koester, Helmut, *History and Literature of Early Christianity Vol.2*. New York: Walter De Gruyter, 1987.

Koestler, Arthur. *The Thirteenth Tribe*. London: Hutchinson & Co. Publishers, 1976.

*Insight Magazine*, "Tracking Mother of 5000 Tongues" by Harvey Hagman, February 5, 1990, pp. 54-55.

Johnson, John L. *The Black Biblical Heritage*. Nashville: Winston- Derek Publishers, Inc., 1993.

LaHaye, Tim and John Morris. *The Ark on Ararat*. New York: Thomas Nelson Inc., 1976.

Latourette, Kenneth Scott. *A History of Christianity I and II*. New York: Harper and Row Publishers, 1975.

Latourette, Kenneth Scott. *The History of the Expansion of Christianity*. New York: Harper & Brothers, 1944.

Lightfoot, Niel R. *How We Got the Bible.* Grand Rapids: Baker Book House, 1963.

Malcioin, Jose V. *How the Hebrews Became Jews*. New York: U.B. Productions, 1978.

Massey, Gerald. *Book of Beginnings Vol.2*. London: Williams and Norgate, 1881.

Massey, Gerald. *The Historical Jesus and the Mythical Christ*. Brooklyn: A&B Books Publishing, 1992.

Mbiti, John S. *Introduction to African Religion*. London: Heinemann Educational Books, 1975.

McCray, Walter Arthur. *The Black Presence in the Bible*, I and II. Chicago: Black Light Fellowship, 1990.

Meinardus, Otto F.A. *Chistian Egypt Ancient and Modern*. Cairo: The American University in Cairo Press, 1977.

Meyer, Robert T., Tranalator. *St. Athanasius The Life of St. Anthony*. New York: Newman Press, 1950.

Mosley, William. *What Color Was Jesus?* Chicago: African American Images, 1987.

Mullins, Eustace. *The World Order*. Staunton, VA: Ezra Pound Institute of Civilization, 1985.

Murphy, Jefferson E. *The History of African Civilization*. New York: Dell Publishing Co. Inc. 1972.

*Newsweek*, "The Search for Adam and Eve" by John Tierney, January 11, 1988, pp. 46-52.

Nietzsche, Friedrich. *The Use and Abuse of History*. New York: The Liberal Arts Press, 1949.

*The Original African Heritage Study Bible*, King James Version. Nashville: The James C. Winston Publishing Company, 1993.

Tresidder, Jack. *The Complete Dictionary of Symbols*. San Francisco: Chronical Books, 2005.

Oulton, John Ernest Leonard and Henry Chadwick, translators. *Alexandrian Christianity*. Philadelphia: The Westminster Press.

Pagels, Elaine. *The Gnostic Gospels*. New York: Random House, 1979. House, 1991.

*Pamphilus, Eusebius. Ecclesiastical History. Grand Rapids: Baker Book*

*Pearson, Birger A. and James E. Goehring, Editors. The Roots of Egyptian Christianity*. Philadelphia: Fortress Press, 1986.

Pentecost, J. Dwight. *The Word and Works of Jesus Christ*. Grand Rapids: Academie Books of Zondervan Publishing House, 1981.

Picknett, Lynn. *Mary Magdalene: Christianity's Hidden Goddess.* New York: Carroll & Graf Publishers, 2003.

*Popular Mechanics*, "Real Face of Jesus" by Mike Fillon, December 2002.

Pritchard, James B. *The Ancient Near East in Pictures*. Princeton: Princeton University Press, 1954.

Radin, Max. *The Jews Among the Greeks and Romans*. Philadelphia: Jewish Publication Society of America, 1915.

Rogers, J.A. *Sex and Race Vol.1*. Petersburg, FL: Helga M. Rogers, St. 1967.

Saakana, Amon Saba, Editor. *The Afrikan Origin of the Major World Religions*. London: Karnak House, 1988.

Smith, Morton. *Palestinian Parties and Politics That Shaped the Old Testament*. London: SCM Press LTd., 1987.

*U.S. News and World Report*, "Who We Were" by William Allman, September 16, 1991, pp. 53-60.

Van Sertima, Ivan and Runoko Rashidi, editors. *African Presence in Early Asia*. New Brunswick, GA: Transaction Books, 1988.

Watterson, Barbara, *Coptic Egypt*. Edinburg: Scottish Academic Press, 1988.

Watts, Daud Malik. *The Black Presence in the Land of the Bible*. Washington, D.C.: Afro Vision, Inc., 1990.

Wells, H.G. *The Outline of History*. New York: The MacMillan Company, 1921.

Wheless, Joseph. *Is It God's Word*. New York: Alfred A. Knopf, 1926.

Williams, Walter. *The Historical Origin of Christianity*. Chicago: Maathian Press, Inc., 1992.

Williamson, G.A., translator. *Eusebius: The History of the Church from Christ to Constantine*. Minneapolis: Augsburg Publishing House, 1965.

Windsor, Rudolphf R. *The Valley of the Dry Bones*. Atlanta: Windsor's Golden Series, 1986.

# INDEX

Made in the USA
Columbia, SC
22 January 2024